Creative Embroidery for Beginners
— a practical guide

French scene.

Creative Embroidery for Beginners
— a practical guide

Anne Coleman

Bishopsgate Press Ltd
37 Union Street, London, SE1 1SE

© Anne Coleman. 1986.

ISBN 0 900 873 78 7 (cased)
0 900 873 79 5 (limp)

All enquiries and requests relevant to this title should be sent to the publisher, Bishopsgate Press Ltd., 37 Union Street, London SE1 1SE

Printed in Great Britain by
Whitstable Litho Ltd., Whitstable, Kent

Contents

1. **Introduction and foreword**   7
2. **Tools and equipment**   9
   a) General
   b) Embroidery frames
   c) The sewing machine
   d) Equipment for design
3. **Useful Techniques.**   25
   a) Transferring designs
   b) Enlarging and reducing designs
4. **Fabrics for embroidery**   30
   a) Background fabrics
   b) Fabric scraps and storage
   c) Colouring fabrics
5. **Threads for embroidery**   42
   a) Collection and storage
   b) Dyeing threads
6. **Colour**   45
   a) The colour wheel
   b) Combining colours
7. **Stitches**   53
   a) An easy stitch: STRAIGHT STITCH
   b) Samplers
8. **Design**   56
   a) What is design?
   b) Collecting ideas
9. **Design based on straight lines**   59
   a) Experiments
   b) Embroidery on stripes 1
   c) Embroidery on stripes 2
   d) Using canvas background
   e) The stitches
   f) Embroidery in stripes 3
   g) Using other materials with canvas
   h) Another easy stitch: COUCHING
10. **Design based on grids.**   71
    a) Experiments
    b) Experiments with fabric and thread

     c) and with stitches
     d) Grid patterns on evenweave fabrics: pattern darning
       and double running stitch.

11. **Associations:** grids and lines and the man made environment   **81**
     A larger project: a house sampler

12. **Stitches**   **87**
     a) More surface stitches
     b) Making use of a stitch dictionary
     c) How to use stitches

13. **Design with curved line**   **90**
     a) Experiments
     b) Experiments with fabric and threads

14. **Associations:** curved line and the natural environment   **94**
     a) Landscape
     b) Small gardens

15. **Shape and form: geometric shape**   **98**
     a) Design with circles
     b) Experiments in embroidery

16. **Associations:** shape and line, colour and pattern and   **102**
     the natural environment
     a) Natural objects
     b) People

17. **Mounting and Presentation**   **108**
18. **Resources**   **114**
19. **Conclusion**   **116**

Introduction

Embroiderers can be divided into two groups. The majority are content to choose and buy a kit, follow the instructions and complete a piece of work which looks exactly like the picture on the packet. They regard embroidery as a satisfying hobby, something which can be taken up for an hour in the evening, a relaxation. The other group take the whole subject much more seriously, and spend as much time on the planning of the design as on the actual sewing. To them it is not a relaxation so much as a way of expressing themselves in fabric and thread, an alternative medium to paint or clay or printing. Increasing numbers of people study embroidery for City and Guilds Examinations, and several universities run degree courses in embroidery.

This book is written for those who would like to begin designing their own embroideries, either because they have tried working an embroidery kit, enjoyed the techniques and would like to go on to creating something more personal, or because they have seen some creative embroidery in an exhibition, or in a book, but do not feel that they have the expertise or the confidence to begin.

Creative embroidery is not difficult but like playing the piano or learning a language, it takes a lot of practice. The reward is being able to produce a piece of finished work which is unique. Nothing can be more satisfying.

Foreword

The first part of the book is taken up with the materials and techniques most commonly used in many embroideries. The collecting of yarns and fabrics is interesting in itself, and there is much to be learnt from just handling ranges of materials, to feel the textures and see the colours and find how they react to one another, what effect they create.

The second part of the book deals with design ideas and stitch techniques. Do not be afraid to experiment with stitch and patterns and with paint and dyes, trying both unusual threads and background fabrics. Experience can be gained which is invaluable when working on something more ambitious. The whole aim is to encourage simple design based on lines and shapes, going on to explore the relationship with similar lines and shapes in the environment, and to encourage an individual style of embroidery through which ideas can be expressed.

Tools and Equipment

Basic equipment for embroidery is simply a needle, some thread and some scissors, but most embroiderers gradually amass a large collection of equipment, fabrics and threads. The following is a basic list which can be added to depending on personal choice.

Needles

A selection of all sizes. In general, needles with sharp points are used on fabrics which are pierced by the needles, e.g. calico, poly-cotton, poplin. Blunt needles are used on fabrics where the threads of the fabrics need to be counted, and the needle passes between the weaves of the fabric, e.g. canvas, evenweave linen, scrims.

There are all sizes of both types, with both long and short eyes, suitable for any thread. The important thing to remember is that the eye is big enough to contain the chosen thread without it constantly slipping out, but on the other hand, not so small that it rubs the thread and frays it. There are needles thin enough to go through small beads, and needles for suede and leather. Keep needles in the packet when not in use, as the paper in the packet is made specially to prevent rusting. Otherwise use a needlecase with flannel leaves. Rough and rusty needles tear fine fabrics.

Go to a large haberdashers to see the selection of needles available. They are sold in sets and in selections of different sizes.

Many people find threading a needle is difficult at first, but this comes with practice; or it might be that the eye of the needle is too small. Many packets of needles are sold with a needle threader, and these are useful.

Pins

Pins have many uses in embroidery, from pinning scraps of fabric to a background to pinning a design onto a fabric. Never leave pins in a piece of work for a long time, as even stainless steel pins can go rusty and mark the fabric.

Scissors

Keep a special pair of scissors for fabric and thread. Ideally it is a good idea to have a large pair for cutting fabrics and a small pair of embroidery scissors with sharp points for cutting threads. Scissors should be sharp. Cutting paper with scissors will blunt them. A good pair of unmaligned scissors will last indefinitely, but if they do need sharpening, have them done at a reputable shop. If you share a house with other people, hide your embroidery scissors!

Tweezers

Useful for holding threads in place, or for placing sequins and beads.

Thimble

Not absolutely necessary, but a thimble protects the finger from being constantly snagged by the needle. It also gives more push to needles which will not easily pierce a thick or difficult fabric. Wear on the middle finger of the sewing hand.

Stiletto

This is extremely useful for making holes in woven fabrics without tearing the threads. Sometimes this is necessary to poke a very thick or inflexible thread through the background. Push the stiletto into the fabric with a twist.

Workbox

These can be found in all shapes and sizes. Although it is a good idea to keep basic equipment in order, do not be in a hurry to buy a container until you know exactly what you will find most useful. Meanwhile, use a shoebox, or a shallow open basket, where everything can be easily seen.

Table

Embroidery has an image of a cosy fireside occupation, but most enthusiasts find they need a table. A functional, plastic topped kitchen table, which can be used for painting as well as sticking and cutting out is ideal. Even a wallpaper table, or a trestle table can be used.

Light

Good light is essential, and an angle arm light is useful for working when others are reading or watching television.

Magnifying glasses

It is best always to work on fabrics where the weave is easy to see, but some people have very poor eyesight. The best sort of magnifying glass clamps to a table, and has a light. These are usually only to be had by mail order, and it is best to send for one where it is possible to send back a glass which is unsuitable. Advertisements appear in craft and specialist embroidery magazines.

A stitch dictionary

Available from the haberdashery department of most big stores, and from craft shops. Choose one with clear diagrams that you can follow easily. (See p. 87).

Embroidery Frames

Some people prefer to hold embroidery in the hand, and some looped surface stitches are not easy to work in a frame. However, it is useful to learn to use a frame for several reasons. First, the frame prevents fabric from puckering or distorting as you sew. Many beginners are disappointed when their first pieces of work are not flat and smooth. Canvas should always be worked on a frame, as it distorts very easily, not because of the embroiderer, but because of the pull of certain stitches. Embroidery techniques where the fabric itself is pulled into patterns by the thread, as in pulled thread embroidery, is almost impossible without a frame. Secondly, a frame can be balanced on the edge of a table, or a chair arm, or it might have a stand or a clamp to hold it on a table, so that the embroiderer has both hands free to work.

Slate frame and Canvas stretchers.

13

There are a number of different types of frame. Choose one which is the most suitable.

Tambour Frames

These are round frames for small to medium pieces of work. These frames are sold in a variety of sizes, ranging from 10cm. to 30cm. in diameter. The tambour frame consists of two rings, one inside the other, and the fabric is held between the two. The outer ring can be adjusted with a screw to accommodate fine or thick fabrics. Tambour frames are made of either wood or plastic, but the wooden frames are best. Bind the inner ring tightly with bias binding, to stop the fabric from slipping or being rubbed by the frame. These frames are not suitable for canvas work.

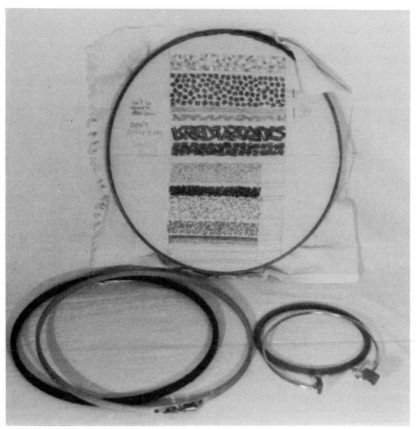

Tambour frames. Machine embroidery ring (bottom right).

Machine Embroidery Rings

These are small plastic tambour frames with a steel inner frame. Sold for machine embroidery, they are very useful for small pieces of hand embroidery, and are easily moved from one area of the work to another. There is no need to bind the inner ring, as the steel is smooth.

Slate Frames

These are suitable for larger pieces of work. The frame is in four pieces, two sides and two ends. The side pieces have webbing tacked down the length. The background fabric is sewn onto the webbing then the excess fabric is rolled up. The two ends act as cross bars, and hold the frame in place. The size of the embroidery is governed by the length of the two sides. These frames can be bought with a stand, or held in the hand. They are useful for large pieces of canvas work.

Canvas Stretchers

These are easy to set up, and cost only a fraction of the price of a slate frame. Canvas stretchers are sold in various lengths and are available from art material suppliers.

The pieces are pushed together at the corners, which are mitred, and can then be wedged. By having two each of several lengths, different rectangles can be made, then taken apart when the work is finished. Tack the fabric to the frame with drawing pins, making sure that there is enough fabric so that the pins do not go through the area which is to be embroidered.

Picture Frames

A picture frame with mitred corners for stability and strength could be used as an embroidery frame. Either pin or sew the fabric to the frame.

Setting up a Frame

The fabric should be taut in the frame, without being distorted.

Leave at least 5cm. spare fabric round the edge. This will be useful later, if the work is to be mounted.

If the background fabric is too small to fit into a frame, machine, or hand sew (in running stitch), onto a bigger piece of fabric like calico or poly cotton. The weft and warp of the fabrics should run the same way. After machining, cut away the calico at the back, up to the machine stitches, or sew through both layers.

Three layers of fabric machined together, some cut away. Applied fringe and machined flowers.

The Sewing Machine

The sewing machine is a useful piece of equipment in embroidery, either as a quick means of attaching fabrics and threads, or as part of the embroidery itself. Many people embroider a large part of the background by machine, then finish off with some hand stitchery. A machine set up for ordinary sewing either straight or zig-zag will make a variety of patterns, just by machining lines in various directions.

Free machine embroidery is also a very useful technique to learn, and worth the amount of time it takes to acquire the technique. Virtually any pattern is then possible.

Free machine embroidery

Can be done on most electric machines and on some treadles, but not on a machine operated by hand. The instruction book will have a section on DARNING or MACHINE EMBROIDERY.

1 Set up the machine as instructed. Make sure the machine is threaded properly, with similar thread in the spool to that on the top. Read the instructions carefully.

   Generally, the foot is removed and the feed dog lowered or covered so that the machine no longer pulls the fabric through automatically, but sews on the spot. Many machines have a darning foot which helps to control the fabric, but it is possible to embroider by removing the foot altogether. It depends on the individual machine.

2 Prepare the fabric by putting it in a small ring. (See p. 19). The ring is important as it holds the fabric taut. Alternatively, the background fabric can be glued lightly to paper. Make sure the glue is dry before working, and that it does not show on the front of the fabric. Paper backed hessian (wallpaper) can be used as background fabric. Use a strong needle.

3 Put the ring, under the needle, resting flat on the base of the machine. Lower the foot, even if the foot itself has been removed.

4 Bring the bottom thread up to the top, by lowering the needle and bringing it up again. Both bobbin and top thread should be on view. Hold them to one side until you have sewn a few stitches then they can be cut off close to the fabric.

5 Start to sew with the needle almost touching the fabric. Hold the ring flat on the base of the machine and move the ring backwards and forwards, evenly. Do not raise the ring or the paper backed fabric towards the needle. Sew as evenly as possible, as jerky movements make the thread break.

   Do not be put off if your first efforts are haphazard, particularly if you are not used to a sewing machine. This technique requires some practice.

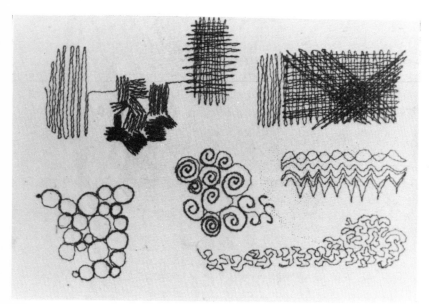

Free machine embroidery patterns.

Machine embroidery – Experiments

Use the machine to try out a variety of fabrics:
1. Make textures and patterns by machining backwards and forwards, round and round to make spirals and circles. Make blocks of colours by machining lines of zig-zag or straight stitch very close together. Make vertical lines, then cross hatch with horizontal lines. Machine over small pieces of stuck on fabric to create areas of colour. Machine on some of the following fabrics to see the different effects: net and tulle, organdie and organza, felt.

2. Machine on two contrasting fabrics held in a ring. (e.g. organdie and net) Machine spirals and circles. Cut away some of the fabric within the circles to reveal the fabric beneath.
3. Machine on two fabrics, the top plain coloured cotton, and the underneath muslin. Make several circles, then cut the muslin and pad the shape out with kapok or stuffing. Sew up the slit. This creates a raised area on the surface. Try out various fabrics with this technique, e.g. knitted fabric, organza etc. Use muslin for the bottom fabric. This is called Trapunto quilting.

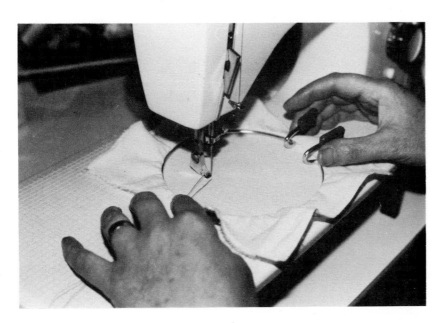

4. Machine together two fabrics with parallel lines of stitches. Thread wool or quilting wool through the channels created. This looks very effective if the top fabric is transparent, and coloured threads are used. It is based on Italian quilting.
5. Machine textures and patterns on plain coloured fabric, then fill in areas of the pattern with fabric paint. Try a variety of machine threads. Many of the more interesting and exciting machine threads are available by mail order and firms advertise in specialist embroidery and craft magazines. Machine embroidery cotton is manufactured in size 30, which is thicker than the threads normally used for dressmaking, and machine embroidery cotton has a high lustre. Silk machine embroidery thread, metallic thread and variagated threads in ranges of lovely colours

19

"Anemones", machine embroidery, free zig zag by MARGARET RIVERS.

20

can also be used. Use the same weight thread on the top and in the bobbin of the machine. Throughout the exercises in this book, use free machine embroidery where it might look interesting or appropriate. Apart from the fact that it is very attractive in itself, it can be combined with hand stitches very effectively, or used to create an interesting background.

Machine embroidery is a technique acquired with practice. Make sure that the machine is threaded properly and that the bobbin is in place and also correctly threaded; that the foot is in the 'DOWN' position; that the machine is set up for darning; that you are not lifting the ring towards the needle. Keep the ring flat on the base of the machine.

If, in spite of practice, the machine still refuses to sew freely consult your nearest stockist.

Equipment for Design

Design is one of the essential elements of embroidery. To start with, a pencil, some paper and some colour, even in the form of coloured pictures from a magazine are all that are really necessary and other pieces of equipment can be added over a period of time.

Paper: Cartridge paper is sold in blocks of various sizes and also in single sheets. Choose a size which you feel comfortable using; many people feel completely outfaced by a large expanse of empty paper. A small pocket sized book (A5 size) is much more useful to start with, and easy to carry about.

Tissue paper in tones of one colour is useful for adding areas of colours or for cutting patterns.

Pencils: There is a large variety of both graphite and charcoal pencils. Start with a medium and a soft charcoal pencil and perhaps three graphite pencils, hard (2H) medium (HB) and soft (4B). These will give a good range of marks. Try them out by doodling, making dots and lines on paper, just to see how they feel, and contrast the marks they make.

Watercolour crayons and pencils, pastels and coloured pencils are also available in a wide range of colours. If possible always try these out before buying, as they are quite expensive.

Pens and ink: Some people enjoy drawing with a biro or a fountain pen, because these are familiar, but coloured inks, drawing pens and fibre tipped pens are also worth trying.

Paints: Many people have a box of watercolour paints left over from childhood, and individual pots of watercolour are available which can be added to these. There is no need to have more than six colours to start with. See page 46 for suggestions.

Poster paint, acrylic or gouache are alternatives to watercolour. It is a good idea to have a small pot of white poster paint for transferring designs. Oil paints are not really suitable for quick colouring exercises, as they take so long to dry.

Paintbrushes: Modern brushes, made from synthetic fibres are both reliable and cheap. It is a good idea to have three brushes, one thick (10 plus) one medium (5 or 6) and one fine (0). The brushes are used for transferring designs, colouring and design exercises and for fabric printing inks and paints. Keep them clean and standing in a jar so that the bristles stay unbent.

Glue is available for fabrics and also for paper. Wallpaper paste is sometimes useful. A tube of glue is more economical than a jar.

Miscellaneous: Scissors for cutting paper. A ruler and a craft knife are all used at various times.

Two pieces of card, cut into right angles (L-shapes) are very useful for looking at parts of a piece of work or a design.

Useful Techniques Used in Embroidery

Transferring a design: There are many occasions when a design needs to be transferred from paper to fabric. The method used depends on how complicated the design is and the type of fabric to be used. Before transferring, the design should be clearly outlined in waterproof ink.

Marking the fabric: Marks made in transferring a design should be as small and insignificant as possible. The marks will later be covered with stitches or removed altogether. There are several methods.

1. A fabric marker is available from large haberdashers and craft suppliers. The marks made are soluble in water, but always test a small piece of similar fabric before using, as fabrics like silk might show a watermark.
2. White or very pale grey poster paint, applied with a fine brush as lightly as possible.
3. Tailor's chalk or pencil.
4. Dressmaker's carbon paper. This can smudge.
5. Waterproof ink can be used on canvas.

Methods of transferring:

1. Window or light box method: Hold the design and fabric to the window. If the lines of the design show clearly through the fabric, use this method as it is very easy.
   a) Tape the design to the window pane, using masking tape.
   b) Tape the fabric over the design making sure that the tape does not come into contact with the area to be embroidered.
   c) Trace the design, using a series of dots.
   A light box can be used in the same way.
2. If the background is opaque and the design is simple, trace the design on tissue paper, pin the tissue paper to the background and stitch along the lines of the design with running stitch. Start with a knot, and use a thread which contrasts with the background fabric. Finish off with two or three stitches worked

one on top of another. Carefully tear away the tissue paper, leaving the stitches to mark the design.

3. A very simple design made up of shapes can also be traced off onto tissue paper., The shapes can be cut out and pinned onto the background. Draw round each one with a fabric marker, or with paint.

4. Dressmaker's carbon paper. Place the carbon paper, ink side down on the background fabric. Place the design on top and pin securely. Draw round the lines of the design with a sharp, hard pencil. Remove carefully. This carbon paper is manufactured in several colours, so choose the palest possible.

5. To transfer a complicated design very accurately to a dark opaque fabric use **prick and pounce.** This is a very old traditional method, which is very dependable. Although it is time consuming, the results are worth the effort, as it is extremely accurate. The pattern can be reused.

   a) Trace the design onto tracing paper. Using a padded surface, e.g. an ironing board, prick along the lines of the design with a darning needle. The holes should be about 5mm. apart.

   b) Turn the tracing paper and using fine sandpaper, carefully sand the holes to remove the nibs of paper.

   c) Pin the background fabric to the board. Pin the design onto the background, making sure everything is firm. Use talc for dark fabric, or if the fabric is white, add a little powdered charcoal to make the powder grey. With a strip of rolled felt, press the talc into the holes.

   d) Gently remove the design. The design has been transferred as lines of dots onto the background. Join the dots with poster or watercolour paint, taking care not to blow away the talc. This is a method reserved for special pieces of work, and should be carried out when you are sure of not being disturbed!

It is very important to make sure that the background fabric is big enough for the design, with enough extra for mounting later on. It is easy to cut away spare fabric, but more difficult to add more (See p. 16). Leave an allowance of at least 5 or 6cm round the edge.

Enlarging or reducing a design

It is often necessary to alter the scale of a design to fit the size required. Perhaps it is a tiny drawing which is to be turned into a wall

Prick and pounce.

Design taken from a photograph.

hanging, or a large photograph which needs to be scale down for a miniature embroidery.

Squaring up and down

The traditional method is to divide the design into squares of equal size then copy the design, square by square to a bigger or smaller guage mesh of squares.

1. Trace the design onto tracing paper.
2. Divide the design evenly into squares, using a ruler.
3. On another sheet of paper, draw out the area of the projected design and divide this into the **same** number of squares.
4. Copy what is drawn in each square of the design onto the empty squares until all the design is transferred.

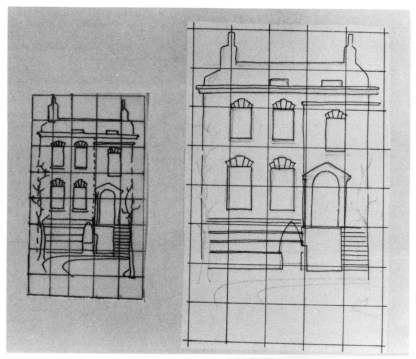

Tracing and enlarging.

Facing page:
Enlarging by photocopying.

Photocopying

The advent of the photocopier with enlarging and reducing facilities has made this technique much quicker and easier for small designs. It is possible to have a design enlarged or reduced exactly to a size within the scope of the photocopier.

Go on to transferring the design to the background using a suitable method. (See p. 25).

Fabrics for Embroidery

Background Fabrics:

Fabrics are available which are specially made for embroidery, and these can be found at specialist craft shops (look in the Yellow Pages) and in some large department stores. Nowadays, many firms sell by mail order, and advertise in craft catalogues and specialist magazines. Local branches of the Embroiderers' Guild and similar groups almost always have supplies of all sorts of fabrics and threads to sell at their meetings.

It is possible to embroider on virtually any fabric, and fabrics sold both for home dressmaking and home furnishing are often most effective.

It is also important to consider what the embroidery is to be used for. Most modern embroidery is made for show, and all kinds of fabrics are used as well as materials like paper, tinfoil and plastic. If the embroidery needs to be laundered regularly, both the background fabric and the threads should be washable.

Whatever the function of the embroidery, the effect the fabrics and threads create is of paramount importance.

Woven Fabrics: These can be divided into two groups.
1. Evenweave fabrics. These are fabrics where the warp and the weft are made up of an even number of similar threads. This creates an even mesh which can easily be seen with the naked eye. These fabrics are used for embroidery where the threads have to be counted accurately so that the stitches make a pattern. Some examples are linen, imitation linen, hardanger, hessian, hopsack which can be used for blackwork, pattern darning; a variety of canvases from very coarse rug canvas to fine linen canvas used for canvas work, and the linen, scrims and loosely woven fabrics used for pulled work. Some dress and curtaining fabric are evenweave and can be used for this type of embroidery. When choosing an evenweave fabric, make sure you can see the individual threads easily.
2. Other woven fabrics which are not evenly woven, or where the threads are too fine to count are used for surface embroidery. Calico, poplin, organdie, fine wool, as well as dress and

furnishing fabric are all suitable, as well as fabrics like chiffon, silk and velvet. Fabrics might be made of natural or synthetic fibres, but always choose a fabric which looks and feels sympathetic to what you are going to do.

Knitted fabrics.

Generally speaking, knitted fabrics (jersey) are not suitable for embroidery as they stretch. However, it is possible in some cases that either hand knitted or machine knitted fabrics might be applied to a background very effectively, for quilting or trapunto quilting.

Felted fabrics

Fibres are treated with heat, water and pressure to create felt, interfacing, paper. Felts, in a variety of colours and weights can be used for embroidery, although felt is apt to stretch. Interfacing is useful for backing fabrics, and iron on and double sided iron-on interfacing can be used for attaching small pieces of fabrics in appliqué. Some embroiderers make paper, incorporating pieces of fabric and stitchery.

To begin: A complete beginner will find it easier to start by using a plain woven fabric, where colour and pattern are added by applying another piece of fabric or by painting or crayoning on the surface before stitching; but to experiment and gain experience, it is well worth trying out a wide variety of fabrics.

Preparation of the background for surface stitchery: As a general rule, always support the background with another piece of fabric like cotton polyester, lawn, well-washed calico or interfacing. This helps to keep the work flat, opaque and gives it more body. This does not apply to embroidery on transparent fabrics, like organdie and chiffon, or to canvas work and counted thread embroidery.

Storage

Background fabrics should be ironed, and stored rolled, rather than folded. Roll the fabric round a core of tissue paper or a cardboard tube. If fabric is folded for some time, the creases are very difficult to iron out, and often attract dirt which is almost impossible to remove. Store the rolls in an old pillow case.

Collecting fabric scraps and how they can be used in embroidery

People who are interested in textiles are apt to collect bags of scraps of fabric both large and small. Some pieces are particularly useful, but it is easy to keep sacks of fabric which are never used and take up valuable space. Experience shows which fabrics will be most useful. Be ruthless with the remainder and throw it away, or give it to someone who might use it.

Fabric Appliqué: This is the technique of applying pieces of fabric to a background to give areas of colour and pattern. The fabrics are either sewn by hand or machine or stuck with fabric glue to create a collage. Some people then go on to add more stitches, while others rely on the fabric to create the effect they want, and add no stitches at all.

Using fabric strips: Woven fabrics can be torn into strips and used as embroidery threads. This can be very effective, and the torn edge gives added texture. Knitted fabrics, suede, leather and felt can all be cut into strips, and used in the same way.

Using strips of fabric as thread. MARGARET RIVERS

Useful fabrics to collect

This is only a very rough guide and it is important to collect only what you are likely to use.
1. Fabrics with small patterns: These can be used for appliqué or patchwork.
2. Pieces of silky, shiny exotic fabrics, shot silks, metallic fabrics, plasticised fabrics. These can be applied as shapes to add richness and texture, or cut in strips and couched onto the surface (See p. 69).
3. Pieces of transparent and translucent fabric like chiffon, organza, tulle. These can be used for areas of colour and layered one over the other. Transparent fabrics can also be rolled and couched onto a background to add a texture.
4. Ribbons, braids, tapes, machine-made laces can all be used either to apply or as threads.
5. Fabrics which fray easily are useful for fringing out to create a texture; for example, some fine tweeds and loosely woven fabrics.

Storage

Like background fabrics, fabric pieces can be ironed, then rolled and tied in bundles. Although the bundles have to be unrolled to find suitable pieces, the method ensures familiarity with each piece, and those which are never used are discarded much more quickly.

Otherwise, fabric pieces can be kept in transparent plastic sacks or stacking boxes. Very small pieces can be kept in plastic sweet jars. Sort the pieces by colour, except for the small patterned fabrics which can be kept separately.

Where to find fabrics

1. Large department stores. Buy as little as 20cm. Browse in fabric and furnishing fabric departments to see what is available. Look at the fabrics closely to see whether they are knitted or woven, and touch them, to see how they feel.
2. Theatrical suppliers. Most of these are in London, but are worth a visit to see the exotic fabrics available.
3. Jumble sales. Look for linen tablecloths and napkins, old chiffon, or silk scarves. **Never** cut up hand embroidery or hand made lace.
4. Mail order. Firms selling bundles of fabric advertise in textile craft magazines.
5. Some small shops, specialising in lampshade making, as well as tailors and dressmakers often sell small bundles of left over fabrics.
6. Furnishing shops and departments sell off samples of curtain and furnishing fabrics in the sales. Some of these are suitable for background fabrics.
7. Embroiderers, Guilds and similar groups have sales tables where fabrics can be bought and exchanged.
8. Small pieces of fabric can also be dyed (See p. 44).

Colouring fabrics

One of the most exciting aspects of modern embroidery is that it is possible to take a plain white fabric, colour it, and then embroider it with threads which have been dyed in exactly the right colour. Some people have always used watercolours, inks and crayons to colour fabrics, but these have not been fast and can fade fairly quickly, or be washed out.

More and more fabric paints and crayons come onto the market each year, and these are stocked by local craft shops and can be had by mail order.

Read the instructions carefully as these products are sometimes made for a particular fabric. However, they are easy to use and very reliable. Most of these paints and crayons are fixed by pressing with a hot iron. It is a good idea to protect the ironing surface with several sheets of newspaper and an old sheet. Some paints are applied directly to the fabric, while others are painted onto paper, then transferred to fabric by ironing.

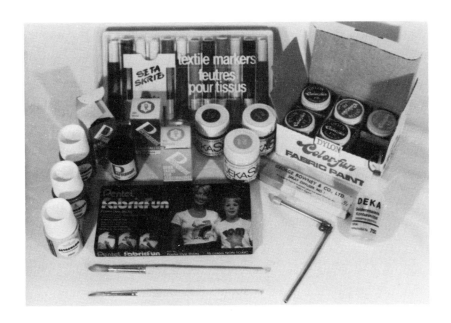

Direct paint

The colour is painted or sprayed directly onto the fabric. The paints are suitable for any fabric and can be mixed together to make more colours (also see p. 46). They are water based.

1. Opaque paint: can be used on both light and dark colours. Some ranges include metallic paint, which can also be used on dark fabric.
2. Transparent paint: can only be used on light coloured fabrics.
3. Silk paints: are very thin and can be used in conjuction with outlining fluid, where areas of the design are outlined and the paint is allowed to flow within the shapes without running into other areas. The paints are also suitable for other fine fabrics.
   Preparation of the fabric: Use a plain, smooth fabric, like poplin, calico, silk, poly-cotton. Some craft suppliers sell fabric which is

already prepared for printing, but many commercial fabrics need to be washed to remove the dressing. Iron the fabric, and tape to a drawing board or a piece of soft board with masking tape. If the fabric is fine enough, the design can be taped underneath, then it can be easily seen, but make sure the design is waterproof.

Painting Methods

Experiment on small pieces of fabric to see the effect of the colours.
1. Painting a background: Areas of fabric can be painted using the paint straight from the jar to give strong, bright colours. Allow each colour to dry before adding another. Details can be added with stitches.
2. Painting on wet fabric: Fabric can be soaked with water, then paint dripped or streaked on to give a watercolour effect.

Left: Areas can be painted. Machine embroidery.

Bottom left: Fabric paint sprayed through net with spray diffuser.

Below: Direct crayons (Pentel) with hand embroidery.

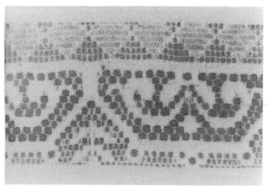

3. Make striped and checked patterns by sticking masking tape across and down the fabric, then painting over. Remove the tape when the paint dries.
4. Paint can be used to add the final touches to embroidery to add more texture and to fill in areas with colour. Use paint and stitches together in some of the exercises on subsequent pages.

Spraying

Fabric paint can be used in a perfume spray or a plant spray, but a spray diffuser, available from art suppliers, is more satisfactory. The paint needs to be watered down. Tape the fabric on a board, and stand the board upright at eye level. Protect the surrounding work area from spray and drips. Spray a fine film of paint onto the fabric. Allow this to dry and spray again, as several fine layers of paint are better than one heavy layer. The paint should not be allowed to run. Using a spray diffuser is a knack; try to blow from the diaphram as if playing a wind instrument. It is also possible to buy an air brush, but these are expensive, unless you are sure it will be used constantly. A car spray is easy to use although it is inclined to stiffen the fabric. These sprays must be used in a well ventilated room.

Spraying methods

1. Stencils: These are cut-out patterns, stuck into position on the background fabric with double sided tape. When the area is sprayed, the stencil acts as a barrier, and the image of the cut-out only is printed on the fabric.
2. Start with simple stencils, like paper doilies, or fold and cut a paper square into patterns. Masking tape can be used as it was with paint.
3. Cut simple geometric shapes, triangles, rectangles from a sheet of cartridge paper, using a craft knife. Both the positive and negative part of the stencil can be used.

Throughout the rest of the book, there are suggestions for pattern making, many of these suitable for fabric printing as well as stitching. Try to keep to simple shapes if these are to be embroidered. The idea is to colour an area which will then be patterned with stitches, but it is possible to find that the fabric prints you do are so attractive, that they stand in their own right without need of further decoration.

Direct fabric crayons are also available, and these are crayoned directly onto a well ironed fabric, taped onto a board.

Transfer paints and crayons

These colours have been specially manufactured for printing on **synthetic** fabrics. A design is drawn out or painted on paper then transferred to the fabric by pressing with a hot iron. It is important that the fabric to be printed is synthetic, or at least contains a high percentage of synthetic, otherwise the colour will not be true. The lower the proportion of synthetic, the lighter the print. Look for synthetic fabrics in any large department store, selling either dress or furnishing fabrics. All fabrics are labelled. Rayon is **NOT** synthetic.

Print onto plain, pale coloured fabrics, as these colours do not print over a dark background.

To make sure results will be satisfactory, do a colour test. This will give an indication of how well the colour prints on the background, as these colours change slightly on transferring, so a test will show the true colour. Using all the paints and crayons one by one, paint a strip of each, about 10cm long, one underneath the other. Cut vertical strips from this to print on a variety of synthetic fabrics. Use thin paper like typing paper.

Protect the ironing surface with newspaper and an old piece of sheet.

Use a non-steam iron if available, as a steam iron has a pattern on the base which can show up in the printing.

The iron should be hot enough to transfer the design, but not so hot that the fabric is burnt. If you are using a test piece, or a small design, cover with another sheet of thin paper, to protect the fabric. Press rather than smoothing.

The design should be well delineated and crisp.

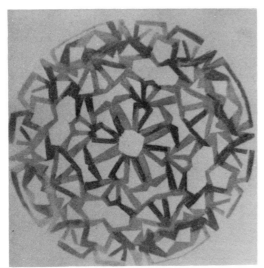

Above: Transfer crayon printed through a stencil, overprinted with flower shapes and decorated with stitches.

Above: Transfer crayon, melted in a folded paper cut out and printed.
Left & top left: Doily and cut out crayoned with transfer crayons.

Transfer Paints

These are very thin, like ink. It is possible to paint a picture and print this onto fabric, but it is much more interesting to create some simple areas of colour and pattern which might then be decorated with stitches.

1. Take prints of leaves and flat seeds. Cover the leaf with a thin layer of paint, and press onto paper. Allow to dry and print.
2. Completely cover a piece of paper by repeatedly dabbing with a piece of sponge, polystyrene or screwed up paper, to make an all over texture or pattern. Tip a little ink into a saucer to dip into. More definite patterns can be made by using a cork, or a rubber or a slice of carrot or a piece of rolled up felt. When dry, these papers can be printed over a stencil or cut up and printed.
3. Completely paint a paper with solid colour. Use this to cut out shapes, which can be arranged and printed. Alternatively, print the colour over a stencil.
4. Paint stripes of colour, being careful to let one colour dry before adding the next. These stripes can then be cut up into diamonds, rectangles, circles, triangles, letter shapes etc. and reassembled in different patterns.

Transfer crayons

Fabric paints are cheap, and appear very easy to use. However, like all techniques, a little care always ensures a very much better result. All crayons splatter, so the design on paper is surrounded by tiny dots of crayon. These will also print, and appear on the fabric, spoiling the effect. Therefore, when working with crayons, **always** cut out the design, and stick it to another piece of paper. Use non-absorbent paper like typing paper.

Because the colours printed are very bright, even garish, more subdued colour can be achieved by printing onto pastel colours like grey, cream, pale blue etc.

1. Take rubbings of natural objects like leaves, dried flowers and flat seeds. Choose shiny leaves, which are more resistant. The back of the leaf will give a better print.

    Rubbings can also be taken of all sorts of textures like embossed wallpaper, bark, fabrics like hessian and nets, anything with a raised pattern. Relief patterns can be created by cutting strips of cartridge paper and sticking these down. Best results occur by not pressing too hard, but trying to create a smooth even layer of colour.

2. Whole areas of paper can be crayoned, then cut out into shapes; folded and cut into patterns, or printed through a stencil. These crayoned papers can also be printed through pieces of loosely woven fabric, or through nets e.g. curtain nets, tulle, hat veiling etc.

3. The crayons need frequent sharpening to maintain a sharp point. Keep the sharpenings, then when quite a lot has accumulated, place in the fold of a sheet of folded paper (non-absorbent). Iron to melt the crayon. This paper can then be cut up and printed, resulting a multi-coloured print.

Some of the methods of colouring and printing are interchangeable, and it is well worth looking out for books on simple printing techniques, even books on printing written for children, for it is often possible to use some of the ideas for making prints on fabric. Books on rubbings are also valuable.

All the colouring and printing described can be done on a small domestic scale, and fabrics can then be printed individually for particular pieces of work.

It is a good idea to try out the different paints and crayons, on a range of fabrics, both white and plain coloured, to get some idea of how they react. These experiments might be quite small, but note how they have been done, and file for future reference.

Tie-dye, batik and space-dyeing. These methods of adding pattern and colour are outside the scope of this book, but are worth investigating as backgrounds for embroidery.

Threads for Embroidery

Always be on the look out for interesting and unusual threads. It is possible to embroider with any thread in some way, and although there are a range of traditional specialist threads, there are also many fascinating yarns which insist on being bought. Traditional threads include stranded cotton, soft cotton, coton-à-broder, coton perlé, tapestry wools, silk twists, and all of these are smooth and suitable for the techniques described in this book. There are also exciting threads which can be borrowed from other crafts: the huge variety of yarns now available for crochet and knitting in all colours and textures; sewing threads in cotton, cotton/polyester and silk and cords for piping; weaving yarns and carpet wools; string and cord used for macrame; very fine ribbons and laces. Parcel ribbons, raffene and glittery Christmas string, as well as a range of twines and strings ranging from very fine and smooth, to very thick and hairy. It is a good idea to go to a large haberdashery department, or better, to a specialist craft shop, and just look at all the yarns which are available.

Notice and compare yarns of the same colour, but made from different fibres and notice and compare the different textures, smooth, slippery, shiny, dull, rough, uneven, multi-coloured. Even strips of fabric can sometimes be used to embroider, giving variation in texture.

Where to buy: Large stores and specialist shops. Many yarn suppliers now deal exclusively by mail order. Address are in specialist

embroidery and craft magazines.

Storage: Try to keep threads arranged so that they can be seen. With a large collection of yarns, it is easy to forget exactly what you have. A collection looks much more satisfactory if the yarns are sorted into colour groups, reds, yellows etc. Plastic sweet jars, often thrown away by shopkeepers make ideal containers because they are transparent, but plastic bags are also suitable. Threads can be subdivided by winding small quantities of yarn round a paper tube, straw or empty cotton reel. Yarns sold in hanks like coton-à-broder and coton perlé can be cut throught the hank at the knot, and three colours plaited together loosely. This prevents the hank tangling up and is easier than winding the whole lot onto an empty cotton reel. Tie the ends of the plait with cotton, to stop it unwinding. Look out for rigid transparent boxes usually used for storage, or for chocolates.

Smooth and slubbed yarns

Threads can be subdivided into two groups, those which are smooth, and those with slubs and snarls spun into them to make a texture. All embroidery where the thread goes in and out of the material, most surface stitchery, canvas work, blackwork and darning, needs a **SMOOTH** thread. Textured threads and metallic threads are attached by couching (See p. 69).

Length of thread

Many beginners use a long length of yarn, which tangles almost immediately. It is much easier to use a short length of thread no more than 50cm, which will not knot or fray against the fabric background.

Dyeing yarns:

A rather drab collection of threads, cheap balls of yarn and left over knitting and crochet yarns in greys, beiges and off white colours which seem unusable at first sight can be totally transformed by dyeing. Many people prefer to dye their own colours and buy only greys in light and dark tones and white, specially for that purpose. Tights also dye well, and can be cut in strips to create yarns.

Requirements for Dyeing

A small tin of hot water (multi-purpose) Dylon dye.
A large pan (rustproof)
Pint Jug
Salt
Rubber gloves
½lb of a variety of yarns (2 or 3 metres of each)

Method

1. Wind the yarn into hanks and tie loosely with a different yarn.
   Have a good variety, remembering that the dye will change the
   colour but not the tone (dark/light) i.e. a dark grey plus red will
   make dark red. A pale colour will not overdye a dark colour.
   Experiment by overdyeing some darker colours, too.
2. Following the instructions on the tin, and wearing rubber gloves,

Requirements for dyeing.

prepare the dye, then enter the yarns.
3. Prod the yarns gently in the dye, rather than stirring briskly.
4. The yarns will be in the water for about 15–20 minutes, and should be moved gently several times.
5. Remove the threads and rinse in plenty of cold water.
6. Squeeze the hanks in an old towel. Do not ring or twist them. Some of the yarns might be wool, or contain a percentage of wool, and too much agitation will felt the wool fibres.
7. Hang the threads in their hanks to dry on a garden cane, or a piece of dowel.

The pan can be cleaned with household bleach.

Notice how some of the yarns have dyed better than others, because of the fibre content of the thread.

The dull collection of yarns will have taken on a much more exciting and homogeneous look and might be used all together for an embroidery, or added to your collection of yarns. Dyes cannot be used satisfactorily a second time, because the salt and dye react together, after which the mixture quickly deteriorates. It is possible to measure out the dye and water solution and the salt, then add a small quantity of each in the right proportion to dye a small amount, or for fabric painting, but this is rather fiddly. Larger quantities of multi purpose dye are also available. It is also worth trying out cold water dye, which is used for natural fibres. Read the instructions on the label.

Many people become interested in dying yarns with vegetable dyes and gain much satisfaction from creating colour from plants, and lichens, etc. Read 'The Use of Vegetable Dyes' by Violetta Thurstan (Dryad).

Colour

Colour has a powerful effect on people, creating moods of happiness, irritation, depression and even fear. For this reason, it is often used deliberately in a society; orange used as a warning; green used as a calming and soothing influence in an operating theatre; red and gold worn by soldiers on parade, the khaki camouflage colours used by a fighting army, and so on. It is interesting to write down a list of the colours of the rainbow with black and white, then to write what each one suggests. Colour is also very personal, and if several people were asked to do the same exercise, their answers would be different. People have 'favourite' colours and many people dislike at least one colour violently. Colour preferences can be seen in other people's choice of clothes and furnishings. Look around and analyse the colours you yourself use, and which colours you avoid.

Colour is one the most important aspects of embroidery. If the colours create the effect you are seeking, the work will have a good chance of being successful.

There are various rules, which are helpful, and mixing paints gives confidence with colour.

Making a colour wheel: The colours of the rainbow are arranged in a circle, making it much easier to see how they relate to one another. Use paint for this exercise, because it can be mixed easily, unlike coloured pencils, crayons or pastels. Watercolour, poster or gouache are all suitable.

You will need the following **PRIMARY** colours. (6)
RED. warm (e.g. crimson) cool (e.g. scarlet)
BLUE. warm (e.g. ultramarine) cool (e.g. prussian)
YELLOW. warm (e.g. ochre) cool (lemon)
Cartridge paper, compasses, pencil, paintbrush.

1. Mixing Secondary Colours (Hues)

All colours can be mixed from the three primary colours, red, blue and yellow. The reason for having a warm and a cool example of each is that no pigment is absolutely pure. For example crimson has a touch of blue, scarlet has a touch of yellow etc. When mixing secondary colours, e.g. orange, the red used should contain a small amount of yellow rather than blue, and the yellow should have a little red rather than blue.

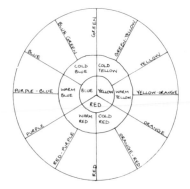

The colour wheel.

46

a) Draw a circle, radius 40cm. with an inner circle of 20cm. diameter.

b) Divide the inner circle into six sections (see diagram) and fill in the warm and cool primary colours.

c) Divide the outer circle into twelve segments. Fill in the primary colours, then mix the secondary colours. e.g. start with crimson, add a tiny spot of ultramarine, so the red is gradually changed to purple.

d) Match yarns and fabrics from your collection with the colours in the circle. Supplement these with strips of colour cut from magazine pictures. Arrange in a circle and stick down.

2. Mixing Tints

Hues can be mixed with white, a little at a time to make a range of tints which go from, for example, crimson through pink to white. Using paints, choose a hue and add white very gradually, to make a range of tints.

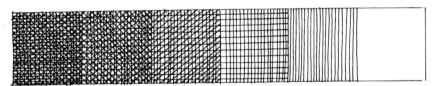

Mixing tints

3. Mixing Shades

In exactly the same way, black can be added to a hue to make a range of dark colours or shades.

4. Mixing Tones

Tones are hues with grey (made from black and white) added. An interesting way of seeing this it to dye a variety of grey yarns in a hue. The result will be a range of yarns in tones of one colour (see p. 44).

5. Mixing Greys

There are many indeterminate colours, greys, browns, beiges, olive, which do not fit into any of the categories above. These are greys or **Greyed colours.** They are the result of mixing the three primary colours, both cool and warm, with each other in various proportions. For example, a high proportion of yellow and blue would give an olive colour, while a high proportion of cool red would give a brown colour. At this stage it is a good idea to make notes of what proportion of each colour is mixed, for some lovely subtle colours can be produced. Always remember that primary colours can be warm or cool, and this also makes a difference to the colours created.

In embroidery, and any other craft where colour is important, the tints, shades and tones of a hue can be used together harmoniously, because all are members of the same primary colour family. However other, more subtle colours (greys) will also harmonise because they also contain a high proportion of that particular primary colour. This gives a much wider spectrum of possible colour choice. It is important to be able to mix colours, so that you can then analyse the obscure and subtle colours of fabric and thread which might occur, and use them to best advantage.

It is also valuable to analyse colours in coloured illustrations, in paintings and other artefacts. Try to mix the same colours in paint and then to match pieces of fabric and threads. All of these ranges of colour can be used in embroidery, not necessarily because they represent anything in particular, but just because they look attractive together.

Autumn study near Oberau by WASSILY KANDINSKY.

48

Looking at The Colour Wheel

Some colours are very bright, insistent, dominant and warm, while others are restful, cool, recessive. It is possible to look at each hue in turn and describe it in words and feelings. In general, the cool colours are grouped together in one segment of the colour wheel, while the warm colours dominate the other. However all hues are more dominant than tones, shades and tints. A hoarding painted in primary or secondary colours will stand out against the surrounding, duller colours, even from quite a long distance. The same is true in embroidery.

Analogous Colours: Any three of four colours adjacent to each other on the colour wheel are called analogous, and harmonise with each other, because they belong to two closely related families. e.g. yellow/yellow-green/green-blue/cool blue. This rule not only applies to hues, but to the tints, tones and shades of the colours, and the greyed colours with a high proportion of the same hue.

Complementery Colours: Colours which occur opposite each other on the colour wheel complement each other. However, they are contrasting, and not related, so they must be used with great care.

Proportion: The amount of colour used is always important. With contrasting colours, a very small amount of one is needed to compliment the other.
   a) Take a range of threads in tones and tints and shades of one colour, then put just a little of the complementary colour with it, then try a large amount. Which do you prefer?
   b) Using strips of paper, cut about 10cm. of a variety of colours. Find the contrasting colour for each, and decide what proportion looks best.
Sometimes only a touch of another colour is necessary. Some colour is bright and strong, some pale and cool. A lot of one colour and a very small amount of another may be needed.
   It is very helpful to look at natural colour schemes, perhaps to find examples of analogous and contrasting colours in nature, as well as ranges of tones of one colour. Look at the subtle colour ranges to be found in stones on a beach, tree barks, mosses and lichens, shells and

stone walls; the rich dark velvety colours in a patch of wallflowers; the luminous metallic colours of the feathers of a flock of starlings. Collect bits of fabric and threads in groups of colours suggested by the things you see.

We are also surrounded by colour in advertising, both in magazines and in displays in shop windows. Colourways in fabrics and colour used in fashion garments and furnishings are all worked out using the principles already outlined, and can be borrowed and used for embroidery.

Look also at the colour used for sets on television, both for plays and magazine programmes, as well as dance and variety programmes. Notice the colour of the clothes of pop groups, singers and dancers, and the colours used for costume dramas and films. Try to decide what you like and dislike and why. It is sometimes enlightening to try out a group of colours which you would never normally consider.

Handling colours in yarns and fabrics and collecting ideas for colour schemes from both the natural and man-made environment gives experience and facility in choosing colour. It also encourages a more relaxed attitude towards embroidery.

Analysing a Painting For Colour

Postcard reproductions of famous paintings are sold in stationers, art suppliers and museums. They are cheap to buy and are often very appealing. Many people collect them as reminders of the real thing. Choose one for its colour
You will need:
Magazines and scissors
Cartridge paper. Paper glue
A range of fabrics and threads in all colours

1. Look at the postcard carefully, and match the colours with the coloured areas in the magazines. Colour samples of paints, available from decorators shops could be used instead of or as well as magazines. Paints can also be used, if preferred.

Colour analysis with yarn and paper.

2. Cut strips of the matching colour about 6cm. long. Indicate the proportion of each colour by cutting very wide or very narrow strips. The proportion is very important.
3. Look for at least twelve colours, even more if you can find them. There might be a whole range of tones of just one colour.
4. Arrange the strips in a column. The pieces might be arranged from dark to light; from dark to light through one colour then back to dark through a second or with the lighter colours in horizontal lines, and the dark colours in vertical stripes, crossing at an angle.
5. Match short lengths of yarn with the colours, and in the right proportion.
6. Does the colour scheme fit in with any of the colour schemes described? Is it analogous, tonal or complimentary?
7. Arrange the picture, the strips of paper and the strips of yarn on a piece of cartridge paper. Stick down. When sticking yarns, it is easier to spread the glue on the background, then press the yarns to the glue. Alternatively, wrap the yarns round a piece of card about 10cm × 4cm.

Other artefacts which are coloured in an attractive way can be analysed in similar fashion: a piece of fabric, a striking advertisement, a colour photograph, a picture in a catalogue, a scarf or a tie, a small natural object like a seedhead, a shell or a flower in a pot.

Look for as many colours as possible, but at least twelve. If the object is three dimensional, the background will also be coloured. Indicate the proportion of each colour as described.

Stitches

An easy stitch: Running stitch, or straight stitch is very easy to work, and can be done almost without thinking about the technique, concentrating instead on creating different patterns and textures.

You will need:
A woven background fabric in a plain colour.
A selection of at least six smooth yarns. e.g. stranded cotton, soft cotton, tapestry wool, cotton perlé, coton-à-broder, smooth knitting and crochet yarns. Choose yarns in a definite colour scheme. e.g. tones of one colour, which match in with the colour of the background. The fabric and threads should look pleasing before commencing.
A tambour frame (about 115cm. diameter)
Selection of needles. Scissors.
Sketch block and pencil.

Starting and finishing: Either start with a knot, or leave an end which can be woven into the backs of the other stitches later. Finish off by weaving into the back of the other stitches. The important point is to make sure the thread is secure. Do not worry about what the **back** of the work looks like, as no one will see it. If the background fabric is transparent, start and finish by weaving the thread into the back of the stitches as neatly as possible.

Make areas of stitch patterns, using two or three different yarns in each area. Different yarns give a variety of textures.
1. Make stitches in blocks, like bricks, keeping the stitches close together. Make some stitches vertical, some horizontal.

MARGARET RIVERS.

53

2. Make a mass of cross stitches, piling stitches on top of one another. Use two or three threads to make contrasts between very fine and thick. Work both even and uneven stitches.
3. Make a sunburst pattern, so that the stitches explode from a centre point. The stitches should be long, short, uneven.
4. Make a scattering of small, short stitches, leaving some as loops, in a pattern like beads dropped on a tablecloth.
5. Starting at one point, work out in a circle, using a variety of yarns, one on top of another.
6. Make an undulating line with stitches, then follow the line along several times until it is thickened and textured.

The idea of these exercises is to see what a variety of patterns and textures can be produced with a single stitch.

This exercise could be done in scores of different ways, using different colour schemes and threads of all kinds.

Always finish each piece of work, making sure enough stitches have been added to make it look rich and interesting. Sometimes the work only begins to look attractive when it is nearly finished. Do not be put off by an empty fabric.

Look as the frontispiece. This is worked entirely in straight stitch, using a variety of stitch patterns.

Part of a Sampler 1650-1700.

Samplers

The simple experiments in straight stitch set out on the previous page are the modern equivalent of the sampler.

In the past, before universal education taught the majority of the population to read, and books became cheap and plentiful, stitches and stitch patterns were collected by embroiderers as reference material. Today, we would use a stitch dictionary. Throughout the past four hundred years, we can see examples of these samplers which are serious collections of stitches, both by professional and amateur embroiderers. Samplers were also made of sewing techniques like buttonholing, patching, gathering etc. Eventually, there evolved the very familiar sampler, which consists of cross stitch patterns, depicting a verse, an alphabet, a name and date. These samplers and others more sophisticated, were worked by women of the middle classes, to show their expertise with the needle. They were started by quite young girls, and provided a pastime for women who were not expected to go out to work, but had to stay at home and do their fancywork. These samplers were made to hang on the wall and be admired.

Today, modern embroiderers still continue to make samplers. As there is now no need to record the actual stitches, since they are printed in so many books, samplers are used as personal experiments in stitchery; trying out patterns of stitches and trying out different threads. There is no longer a real need to decorate clothes and furnishings by hand, as this is done so much more quickly and cheaply commercially. The way the stitches are used expresses the individuality of the embroiderer, using fabrics and threads as an art medium, like paint or clay. Samplers reflect the social lives of the people who work them.

The state of embroidery as an art and the way it is viewed by society is found in the types of samplers which have been done, and are still being worked today.

Samplers have a great fascination for collectors, and command high prices in the salerooms. Many local museums have well documented examples of the various types, and there are several interesting books on the history of the sampler. Keep your own samplers as reference material. Any particularly successful examples can be mounted as a picture.

Design

What is design

Design, colour and technique are the three important components which go together to make a successful embroidery. Making patterns with stitches creates accidental design which can be very attractive and give ideas for more work. However, most people who learn to embroider also want to learn how to design; often something specific. They want to learn how to turn what they can see and feel into embroidery. Like working with colour, this becomes easier with practice.

Design is often confused with drawing, but designing really means looking, choosing and recording. Looking at colour, shape, texture, pattern, choosing from the mass of information which parts are really relevant, then recording in fabric and thread. It also means experimenting with stitches, to see what patterns and textures they produce, learning which colours express which ideas in the best way and choosing the most suitable fabrics and threads to use. In short, bringing colour, design and stitches together into an embroidery. The design is a working plan, used as a pattern to create an embroidery. It will consist of an overall master-plan which has been worked out from sketches, collages and photographs with indications of the finished size. Stitch experiments, colour schemes and samples of suitable materials are all relevant. Never throw away any preliminary work, but keep everything together in a plastic wallet. Never cut up the master plan itself, but take a tracing and cut that instead.

The design must be completely satisfactory before beginning the final embroidery, even though it might take a long time to work out exactly what is wanted. Some people take months or even years to mull over an idea. The final embroidery should be easy. There should be no problems because all these have been worked out beforehand. For this reason, many people prefer to work on several ideas at a time.

However, one of the fascinating aspects of embroidery is that along the way to a finished piece of work, it is possible to be diverted into the creation of stitch samples, and experiments in colour and texture, which are satisfying in themselves. Some people get so caught up in preparations and try-outs that they never get round to

56

finishing anything very big. On the other hand, other people launch straight into the embroidery with little preparation on paper, as if the design and samples were already imprinted on their brain. It does not really matter. You choose the way which is best for you. This book only suggests an outline of the way things might be done.

Collecting ideas

It is a good idea to get into the habit of collecting ideas which appeal to you for eventual interpretation in embroidery. It might be anything and individual people are interested in many and diverse things. There is no reason why you should not embroider anything at all, from machinery and multi-storey blocks of flats to people, seascapes and beds of flowers. The pattern created by books on a bookshelf might appeal to one person, while another is excited by the textures on a stone wall. Never be put off if you really want to embroider something specific.

1. Drawing: Try to draw, even if you think you cannot, because it is a valuable aid to embroidery. The drawing itself is not so important as the fact that you are forced to look carefully at an object and analyse what you see so that it can be recorded. Buy a small cartridge block, which can be carried round all the time. It is easier to draw with a fairly soft pencil (2B,4B). Start by making marks, in the same patterns suggested for stitching. (See p. 53), then go on to drawing small things; a leaf, your finger nail, a jar. Look at the overall shape,

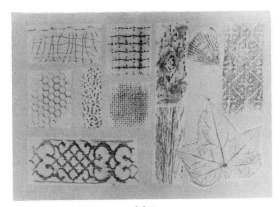

Ideas for design: rubbings.

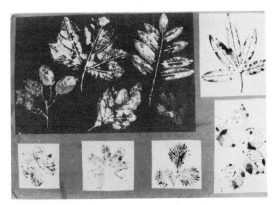

Ideas for design: prints with paints.

then follow right round it with your eyes. Draw it in the air first, just over the paper, but without touching. Draw some of the pattern you see on the object. Choose one small area, and draw what you can see. The page might be just fragments of pattern, texture of the same object. Go on to using water-colour pencils and crayons, charcoal pencils and pen and ink. All these give a different effect.

2. Paper cutting and tearing: Cutting and tearing paper can produce patterns which might be interesting as a basis for design and embroidery. There are several different papers which can be used and all give a different result. Try out tissue paper, brown wrapping paper, coloured paper. Paper can be folded and cut, or simply torn into shapes.

3. Photography: Even a very simple automatic camera will take a record, which can be used as a reference. Always get as close as possible to what you want to photograph, filling the view finder. Take photographs of man-made patterns on stone, wood carving, machinery as well as natural patterns on plants and animals. Take groups or collections of objects, piles of wood, rows of pots, rows of plants. If you are taking a photograph of a landscape, take several, then make a panorama. As soon as the photographs come back from the processor, write your ideas on the back, or they will be forgotten.

4. Photographs and postcards: Collect photographs from magazines and buy coloured postcards. Try to decide what you like about that particular picture, whether it is the pattern, the colour or the composition which is appealing. Keep a folder of these cuttings and pictures, and go through them from time to time, as they might suddenly have relevance to what you want to do.

Design based on Straight Lines

This is an easy way to start building up design patterns, and by using different colour schemes and using other media like coloured paper, it is possible to make a number of variations.

A simple experiment with a sheet of file paper

You will need:
One sheet of ruled paper, a ruler and a pencil.
The lined paper is designed to keep writing evenly spaced and neat. It does not appear to be a very exciting embroidery design at first sight.

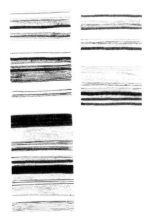

1. Make four boxes, about 4cm. wide and 10 lines deep, using the pencil and ruler.
2. In the first box draw horizontal lines, **freehand** (the ruler is only for drawing the boxes). Some lines should be close together and some wide apart to make an uneven pattern of stripes. When you are satisfied with the first, go on to filling in the other three. Each should be different.

What has been created from an area of ruled paper is design based on horizontal lines or **STRIPES**. Because the spaces are now uneven, the designs are much more interesting for embroidery or striped fabric or wrapping paper, but no longer suitable for writing paper. Good design should be functional.

Making stripe designs

You will need:
Cartridge paper, pencil and ruler. Scissors.
A selection of paints, crayons, inks, wax crayons, coloured paper and glue, tissue paper, magazines.

1. Draw four or five boxes with the pencil and ruler, about 7cm. by 12cm. (The size of a design, or an embroidery is a matter of personal choice. Some people prefer to work on a very small scale and some on a large scale, so all measurements mentioned can be changed).
2. Go on to filling in each box with parallel horizontal lines, using some or all of the media mentioned, either separately or together. Also think of the effect of the colours.
   a) Use a wax crayon to draw lines, then paint over the lines, so that the wax resists the paint.
   b) Stick strips of paper, both tissue and coloured, super-imposing some strips over others, or use coloured strips from magazines.
   c) Paint lines, then draw more lines with ink
   d) Draw with coloured water-colour crayons on a wet surface.
   As you draw, think of the pattern the lines and spaces are creating.
Concentrate on each design and do it as well as possible. It soon becomes clear that some of the designs are better than others, and that the actual practice of drawing and colouring encourages new ideas and different permutations.

At the same time, begin collecting examples of striped designs like wrapping paper, fabric, wallpaper, patterns on china, patterns on buildings. Collect postcards and magazine pictures and take photographs.

Embroidery on stripes 1.

Stitches can be used as texture to decorate a striped fabric background. Very different impressions can be made by using a variety of:

Backgrounds: Try some of the following:-

1. Striped fabric: choose a fabric with printed stripes in one or two

colours. Threads can then be chosen to match the colours. Some Indian cotton furnishing fabrics have woven stripes, either self coloured or with a matching woven coloured stripe. These fabrics are easy to decorate, using the stripes as a guide.

2. Hand printed fabric: Print a striped fabric, either by using fabric paint or transfer paint and masking tape or stencils. (See p. 37).
3. Create a striped background by machining ribbons and strips of torn fabric across a plain coloured background.
4. Choose unusual background materials which already have lines of holes which can be threaded to make stripes; nets like coarse hat veiling, vegetable nets, sequin waste, loosely woven curtain fabrics.

Choose fabrics where the weave can be seen easily as a guide.

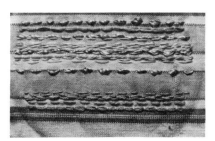
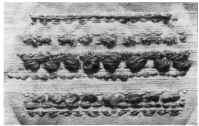
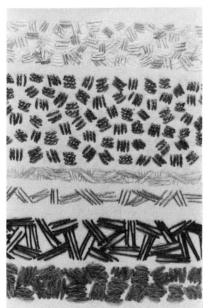
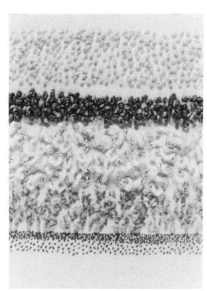

Yarns

Use a good range of threads, both commercial and home-made. Look for contrast in the threads you choose: thick and fine, shiny and dull, hairy and smooth. Be sure they do not contain snarls and slubs.

Stitch across the fabrics following the lines, using the stitches to add texture to the stripes.

Some areas should be thickly textured, while some areas should be sparsely spotted, or left completely empty. Some stitches should be large, some small, some even, some uneven. Stitches can be left as loops on the surface.

Use double or quadruple yarns to make really thick stitches. Forget about the sort of neat little stitches you might use for hemming an edge and really try to make the samplers look exciting and richly textured. Add shine and glitter with silver and gold metallic thread.

This exercise, and those on the following pages show how easy it is, when using simple designs and stitches on a variety of background fabrics to create very effective pieces of embroidery.

Embroidery on stripes 2.

Looking back at the first sampler on p. 53 and the frontispiece the patterns were made by stitching in different directions. Some were all vertical, some horizontal some criss-cross, diagonal, in blocks, in scatters etc. The stitches gave both pattern and texture.

By combining directional stitch patterns with some of the striped designs, another sort of pattern is created.

To make a sampler you need:
One or two pieces of plain coloured fabric; poplin, washed calico, silk. Back with cotton fabric to support.
A range of smooth threads, stranded cotton, cotton perlé, knitting yarns, raffia, tapestry wool, sewing cotton etc.
Fabric and threads should be in matching or toning colours.
An embroidery ring, needles, scissors.
A fabric marker and ruler.
Sketch book and pencil or pen.

1. On the fabric, mark out a box about 16cm. × 12cm. (or a size

which fits in the embroidery ring).

2. Divide the rectangle horizontally into stripes (copy one of your successful designs).
3. Choose **one** directional stitch pattern.
4. Use this stitch pattern to decorate some of the stripes, using the pattern with different threads.

Some stitches might be very thick, very fine, worked in several yarns, using large stitches, using small stitches.

Leave one or two stripes empty for balance and contrast. Some stripes should be heavily patterned and dark, while some might be quite lightly patterned.

It would be possible to go on to do several completely different samplers, each using the one directional pattern, but depending for variety on the colours, the backgrounds, the contrast between light and dark areas.

It is a good idea to try out different directional patterns on paper, with pen or paint, just to see the great number of different possibilities.

Variations

1. Similar samplers might be made using either a commercial or a hand printed striped background.
2. Paint some of the stitch patterns with fabric paint, mixing painting and stitching.

Using a canvas background

Canvas work is an embroidery technique which many people enjoy exclusively. Many commercial embroidery kits or 'tapestries' are actually canvas work, and very often these kits make extensive use of a stitch called PETIT POINT or TENT Stitch. This little stitch will cover a surface with a fine, smooth area of colour and is very attractive. There are also a very large number of alternative canvas stitches, however, which are easy to do and which make some lovely textures and patterns.

The canvas

Canvas is a stiffened, even-weave mesh, made in various sizes ranging from rug canvas to fine linen canvas. It is measured by the number of threads to 2.5cm. of canvas. Canvas is manufactured in **double** or **mono**.

Double canvas is used for work which is trammed. i.e. a long thread is taken right across from one side to the other, then covered with a line of cross stitches, and the extra yarn gives a denser finish.

Mono canvas is much easier to use, particularly for a beginner, and is recommended for the work in this book. Double canvas can also be used as mono, by only sewing into each alternate hole. This is useful on a large panel, where most of the background can be worked using every alternate hole, but fine details like faces and hands can be worked in a finer yarn, using every hole.

Canvas is made from a number of fibres.

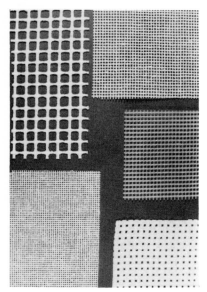

A variety of canvases including cross stitch canvas (Binca).

Free straight stitch horizontal and vertical.

The yarns

Any smooth thread is suitable, as long as it covers the canvas satisfactorily, to give an even surface with no distortions. The canvas is covered with no gaps between stitches.

1. Tapestry wool: This is manufactured specially to use on canvas. It is sold in skeins, some stranded into six threads. The colour

64

range is excellent. There are several different makes.

2. Knitting and crochet yarns: These are suitable if they are smooth and fit in with the other yarns in weight. Fine yarns can be doubled if necessary.
3. Carpet thrums: can be bought from **carpet mill** shops and by mail order. These are the ends of wool used to weave carpets, and although they are rather coarse, can often be had in a good range of subtle colours.
4. Embroidery threads, soft cotton, cotton perlé, silk twist, stranded cotton are all suitable, particularly for fine canvases. They also give contrast of texture when used with wools.

Points to remember

1. Use a frame for all except the smallest pieces of work, as canvas stitches can really distort a canvas.
2. Always make sure the yarn used is thick or fine enough by doing a test piece of about 4 to 5cm. square.

The Stitches

The great majority of canvas stitches are based on straight stitch, (flat stitch) either worked in various directions, or crossed. The stitch patterns are made by counting the threads and making a small area of pattern, which can be repeated to make lines of pattern or an all-over pattern.

It is also possible to cover an area of canvas with irregular straight stitches worked in different directions.

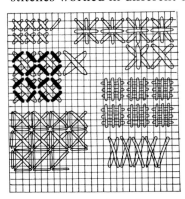 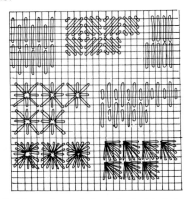

Canvas stitches based on cross stitch (left) and straight stitch (right).

The same stitches can be worked on any size of canvas, using a suitable yarn.

Experiment on offcuts of two or three different sized canvases, e.g. rug canvas (approx 20cm. sq.) size 10 (approx 16 × 14 cm.) and size 19 (approx 6 × 8cm.). Use a variety of smooth yarns, to see how each one works, perhaps using double or treble yarns for the largest mesh.

There is no need to put test pieces in a frame, but tape the edges of the canvas with masking tape, to prevent fraying. Use a tapestry needle of the correct size for the yarn used, and use only a short length of yarn (about 30 cm.).

At the beginning of the work, leave an end which can be darned into the back later on. Finish in the same way.

Embroidery in stripes 3.

A canvas work sampler.

Stripes are an excellent design source for canvas work, as most of the stitches can be worked out easily in lines and blocks. The stitches themselves dictate the width of each stripe, which might be a single, double or treble row of each stitch pattern. Let the lines of stitches contrast with each other in texture, using a highly textured stitch next to a fairly flat stitch, a dense stitch next to a sparse stitch etc.

Some stitches can be worked in two contrasting yarns, (e.g. tapestry wool and perlé) one half in one, one half in the other.

Choose a colour scheme, but beware of too much colour with a variety of canvas stitch patterns, otherwise the effect can be rather cluttered. Tones of one colour or at most analogous colours look lovely. When using a wide range of colour, only use one or two stitches, although this is a matter of personal taste.

The sampler

You will need:
Canvas.
Smooth yarns, tapestry, perlé, knitting wool.
Frame, scissors, tapestry needles.
Graph paper and pencil.

1. Decide on the design. This depends on the stitches to be used. Use the stitch samplers you have done, and work out in which order the stitches will come and how many lines of stitches will make up

each stripe. Use the graph paper to record this. Work out the size of the finished piece.

2. Tape the edges of the canvas, either with fabric tape for a slate frame or masking tape for a frame made of wooden stretchers. Fix the canvas in or on the frame. It should be taut, but not distorted. Remember to leave a border of at least 5cm.

3. Assemble the yarns, making sure they look attractive together. Decide which yarn is to be used for each stripe. Although this design is being considered on size 10 canvas, it could be carried out on any size, large or small, using the correct weight yarns. Always start by doing a test piece,
   a) to see what area the design will cover and to estimate the amount of yarn you will need for the whole piece, and
   b) To make sure the yarns are suitable for the background canvas. By covering a canvas with stitches, a fabric is created. Depending on size and weight, this might be used for a wall panel, a rug, or to make an artefact like a bag, a purse, a seat or a cushion.

Only when making something which is to be worn is it necessary to use conventional materials.

 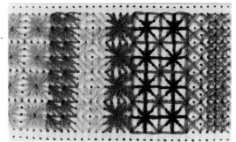

Sampler on No. 10 canvas.   *Sampler on a Binca canvas.*

Using other materials with canvas

Canvas need not only be used for counted stitches. When combined with other techniques, canvas work can be both exciting and innovative. The canvas itself is a very strong, firm background, excellent for applying other materials.

The following suggestions are just a few ways in which canvas can be used.

1. Areas of canvas can be painted, then patterned with stitches. Some people like to add colour as they sew. Use fabric paint.

67

2. The canvas itself can be used as a stencil to print on another fabric, which can then be decorated further with stitches.
3. Applying fabric:
   a) Small pieces of coloured fabric like net, chiffon, organza and organdie can be applied to the canvas, and stitches can then be worked through the fabric into the canvas, giving a rich exotic effect.
   b) Small pieces of hand knitting can be applied, to cover some areas. The yarn used to knit can then be used to fill the areas of uncovered canvas with stitch patterns.
4. Ribbons, strips of fabric and raffia can be used as effectively as the more usual yarns, giving thick textures. Leave some of the ribbons looped on the surface of the canvas.
5. Canvas patterns or motifs can be inlaid in another fabric using the technique of **reverse appliqué**. Pattern an area of canvas with stitches, then take the other fabric and sandwich the two together, right side of canvas to **WRONG** side of the fabric. Turn and machine round the motif on the canvas side. Turn and cut away the fabric from the canvas stitches, up to the machine stitches.

   This technique can be carried out using line or grid patterns. Sandwich canvas with another fabric, and machine lines and grids on the canvas side. Turn. Cut away the fabric in parts, and pattern the areas of canvas revealed with canvas stitches. Fabrics like felt and velvet are effective for this technique. Use a straight stitch for felt, close zig-zag for velvet and other fabrics.
6. Rug canvas can be machined with zig-zag worked over the weft and warp of the fabric to create lovely colour changes. e.g. work vertically down each warp thread in turn, starting with a pale colour on the first and gradually changing to darker and darker colours. Turn the canvas and work across the weft threads in the same way.

 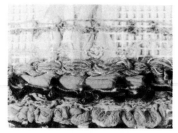

Canvas can be stitched and threaded with thick yarns, plaits, fringes and strips of fabric. MARGARET RIVERS.

Another easy Stitch: COUCHING

It must be obvious by now that the number of stitches used in embroidery is not important, but the stitch textures, colour combinations and patterns are. Straight stitch is enormously versatile, because it is easy and natural to work without having to concentrate too much on the technique, but thinking instead of the many different ways in which it can be used.

However, some yarns are not suitable for stitching through a fabric, because they are so textured that they will not pull through the background without unravelling, or at least being pulled out of shape. This also includes silver and gold threads, ribbons, plaits and braids which are too bulky to stitch through a fabric.

Couching overcomes these difficulties because the yarn is only pushed through the background fabric at the beginning and end of the work, and is held down on the surface by smaller stitches in a matching fine yarn.

To try the technique:

You will need:
An embroidery ring and background fabric in plain-coloured woven fabric.
Thick knobbly threads, plaits, metallic threads. Matching sewing cotton and needle.
A stiletto, scissors, fabric marker.

1. Mark out a simple line design on the fabric. Always mark the design on the fabric rather than trying to pin down the yarns.
2. Push the point of the stiletto into the fabric at the beginning of the design. Twist down into the fabric, taking care not to tear the weaves.
3. Push the end of the material to be couched through the hole push the weaves back into place.
4. Follow the design with the yarn to be couched, oversewing every so often with the matching sewing cotton.
5. To finish off, make another hole with the stiletto and push the end of the couched thread through. Catch the ends of the couched yarns down to secure in position.

Variations

1. Use a contrasting instead of a matching cotton to attach the couched thread.
2. Make a definite pattern with the thread used to attach the couched yarn, perhaps using a thicker smooth thread.
3. Whole areas can be filled with couched yarns. This can be seen in ecclesiastical embroidery in churches, where gold threads are used on rich background fabrics in beautiful line patterns and filling stitch patterns.
4. A suitable printed pattern can be accented with a couched thread.

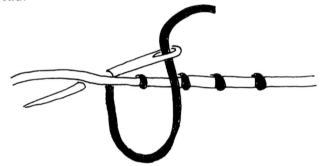

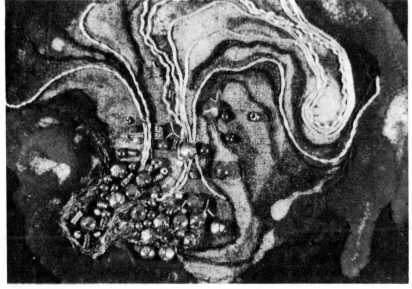

Couching on marbled fabric.   *MARGARET RIVERS*

70

Designs Based on Grids

We have been considering designs based on straight lines, stripes of colour and stitch texture and pattern.

If horizontal lines are crossed with vertical lines, a grid is formed and a whole new area of design ideas is created.
These grid patterns:

1. Cover an area with pattern.
2. Produce patterns which can be used to fill a particular shape.
3. Produce geometric shapes like diamonds, squares, rectangles and triangles.

Try some experiments on paper:
You will need:
Pencils, crayons and paint.
Cartridge paper, tissue paper and one or two pieces of stiff coloured paper about 15cm. square.
Scissors, glue, ruler, craft knife.

1. Make grids, both with and without a ruler, using soft pencils, coloured crayons or paint. Think of all the possible patterns using horizontal, vertical and diagonal lines, both evenly and unevenly spaced.
2. Fill in some parts of the design in the central area of each grid OR evenly all over with colour, or with pencil lines etc. Make use of interesting colour schemes, perhaps using tones of one colour in one or two contrasting areas, or gradually darkening a colour from one side of the work to the other, or using only greys with black and white.
3. Cut or tear strips of tissue paper, coloured paper or pictures from magazines and make grid patterns. Fill in some of these and decorate with pencil and crayon.
4. Completely cover a sheet of cartridge paper with colour; by painting areas and allowing the wet paint to run together or by sticking strips or areas of coloured tissue paper to cover the paper completely. Draw a grid over the top, cut out the shapes and stick down on another piece of paper, perhaps coloured, leaving a space between each shape.
5. Use a craft knife to cut a shape out of the centre of the stiff

coloured paper. This could be a geometric shape like a circle or a rectangle, or a window shape, or an archway. It might be the simplified shape of a flower or butterfly or a leaf. Place the cut-out over some of the grid patterns. Use the shapes cut out of the card and place **ON** various patterns to show the effect of a patterned background.

These exercises show how an area might be covered with pattern, how a definite shape might be patterned or how a background might be patterned.

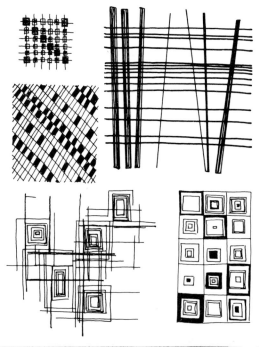

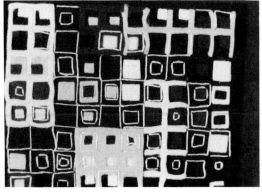

Experiments with fabric and thread

While exploring ideas on paper and using paint, crayons and pencils, it is also profitable to design **directly** with fabric and thread. These are experiments and at this stage, it is better to try out different fabrics, yarns and materials on a small scale, rather than spend a lot of time and effort on only one piece. The work produced is for reference. However, any of these trial pieces might give ideas which could lead to a more ambitious piece of work.

Always choose fabrics and yarns which look harmonious for each piece of work, however small. This is an opportunity to try out different and unusual colour schemes.

1. Using masking tape, build up a grid pattern on a suitable fabric, then colour with fabric paint. Some strips of tape might be narrow some wide. Vary the spaces between the strips. When the fabric is fixed, decorate with:
   a) Yarns couched along between the lines of the design or by
   b) Filling some of the spaces with stitches or by
   c) Sewing ribbons and braids across and down.
2. Using a sewing machine, make a grid pattern, sewing through two, three or four layers of fabric, sandwiched together. Fabrics should be securely held in place with pins. Cut away some of the shapes to reveal the fabric underneath. Fill some of the shapes with stitches and beads. The interest comes with the sorts of fabric used and the combinations of fabric. There are some lovely metallic fabrics, shiny satins, shot silks and organzas which are excellent for this type of work. Do not use large patterned fabric, the effect of which would be lost, but use plain or small patterned materials.
3. Use a piece of woven fabric in a plain colour and
   a) Sew ribbons across and down, using a sewing machine and either straight or zig-zag stitch, using a variety of machine threads, including metallic and variegated.
   b) Use strips of cut felt or strips of torn or rolled organza, organdie, chiffon or tarletan.
4. Using fabric glue sparingly, stick scraps of fabric either in stripes or in areas of colour onto a firm fabric background like poplin or calico. With a sewing machine, zig-zag across and down to create a grid pattern. Some of the lines of machine stitches might be quite close together. A zig-zag can either be open, so that the background shows through, or closed to make a line of satin

stitch, so try both ways.

These exercises often provoke other ideas, which you should try out. Always be willing to experiment with your own ideas.

Experiments with Stitches

Couching and straight stitches can be combined to make grid patterns which fill an area with decoration. These filling stitches can be made by criss-crossing an area with long threads, which are couched at the intersections, and can either be regular or irregular. Some, or all parts of the grid can then be decorated further with stitch patterns, again either regularly in every space or every alternate space for example, or irregularly in one area. Horizontal, vertical and diagonal lines can be used, as well as straight lines at any angle to make a variety of interesting and contrasting patterns.

Notice also the **OVER-ALL SHAPE** the whole pattern makes on the fabric. This should also be balanced. Make several small samples. Each should look attractive in itself. For one sample you will need:

Plain coloured woven background fabric and a variety of smooth yarns, fine ribbons, cords, metal threads etc. to match in together.
An embroidery ring.
A fabric marker, needles, scissors and stiletto.
Paper and pencil.

1. Draw out some ideas on paper, or use some experimental ideas from the previous pages.
2. Mark out the area the embroidery is to cover on the fabric, and mark in the grid pattern, or just copy it straight onto the fabric with stitches.
3. Couch down the grid pattern. Use a matching or contrasting variety of threads to decorate some of the spaces created. Pick up the shapes the grid makes (squares, triangle, diamonds etc.) for the decorative pattern. Fill in either regularly, in every or every alternate space, or irregularly in a cluster.

   Make several small samples, trying to make each as interesting as possible, and try to do at least one example of both a regular and irregular pattern.

   Use contrast in the texture of the threads and the couched threads making use of metallic thread, matt threads, shiny and dull threads etc. Contrast light areas and darker shapes, balancing these to give an all over effect that is attractive. Some areas might be densely packed with stitches, while others are sparse and light.

These samples show how many different effects are possible with one or two stitches.

Never be afraid of altering the original design as you go along if you think it would look better slightly differently, or indeed of experimenting with your own ideas. Embroidery is a very personal statement and the results should be satisfying to you and not necessarily a carbon copy of what someone else tells you to do. One of these samples could be worked on a large scale, giving scope for more detail in the patterned areas.

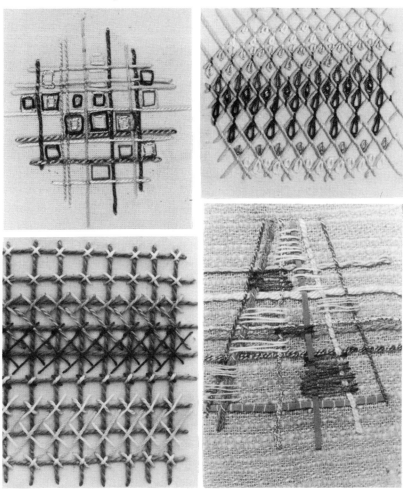

Weaving and Counted Thread Experiments

There are a great variety of nets and meshes, vegetable bags with square and diamond mesh, hat veiling, sequin waste and many knitted mesh fabrics, sold for exotic evening wear. All of these are knitted or woven on a grid pattern, some with square or triangular mesh, occasionally hexagons.

1. Smooth yarns and ribbons can be threaded through the mesh, diagonally or from top to bottom and side to side. These can be
   a) irregular, threading to make an interesting texture rather than a pattern, or
   b) regular, counting the threads and weaving to make a neat pattern.
      When trying this technique, always use a frame. The fabric could be pinned out on canvas stretchers or held in a tambour frame. It is almost impossible to count the threads and holes if the material is hand held.
2. Ribbon weaving gives a pretty result, and ribbons can now be found in various widths and all colours. Strips of torn fabric or cut fabric frayed out on each edge could be used, as the frayed edge gives a good texture.
   Hold down ribbons horizontally on a piece of soft board, by pinning at each end, one directly below the other.
   Weave the vertical ribbons through, and hold them in position with a pin at each end as they are woven.

The woven piece is held in position by machining across the ends, or by hand stitching.

3. Use rug canvas which has square mesh and is nice and stiff and easy to use.

    a) Weave strips of ribbon, rug wool or torn fabric in and out to make a regular pattern

    b) Wind separate yarns down each of the warp threads, going round each intersection once. In the same colour order, wind across each weft thread, again, using a separate thread. This creates interesting colour changes as the threads cross. Try a colour scheme from dark to light, or from one colour to another, graduating through the intervening hues.

Grid Patterns on Evenweave Fabrics

1. Pattern Darning

Even-weave fabric is made up of a mesh of horizontal weft threads, and vertical warp threads. Patterns can be made by darning under and over the threads of the background fabric, either horizontally or vertically. By counting the threads, regular geometric shapes can be built up, for example, diamonds, triangles, chevrons, rectangles etc.

Refer back to the STRIPED patterns created by drawing, painting and sticking paper, for these can be used as a basis for designs for pattern darning. The designs can be transferred to graph paper.

To try this technique, you will need:
Several striped designs, about 4cm. deep and 20cm. long.
Scissors and graph paper.
Cut each of these into regular geometric shapes, diamonds etc.
Arrange in a line with a space between each, and stick down.
Transfer to graph paper.

Pattern darning is a very simple technique, made exciting by the threads and colours used. The threads are darned through the fabric in a pattern, copying the pattern on the squared paper.
You will need:

Evenweave fabric. Make sure the holes can be seen easily.
Yarns. Choose colours to match your design as nearly as possible. The yarns should be smooth, and about as thick as the threads which go to make up the background fabric. Include yarns like wool, silk, cotton, shiny yarns, metallic yarns.
A tapestry needle.
Refer to the design. Work from right to left.

Weave each thread through the fabric, counting the threads, and following the weave of the fabric.

Each individual thread in the design should go right across the width of the fabric. One horizontal line of squares on the graph paper represents each individual thread darned across. When the whole design is worked, it can be repeated to form a block of pattern.

Pattern darning can be worked vertically, horizontally or a mixture of both, and will form a large variety of simple or quite intricate patterns.

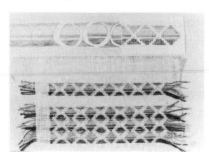 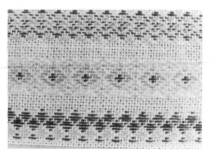

2. Double Running Stitch

In pattern darning, lines of darning stitch are built up to form coloured blocks and patterns. Double running stitch can be used in a very similar way, to build up patterns in **one** colour on a contrasting coloured fabric. e.g. black on white, white on colour etc. The patterns are based on squares, diamonds, triangles, hexagons. To make patterns based on squares, you will need:

A piece of evenweave fabric with a very clear weave, **OR**
A piece of Binca canvas. (cross stitch canvas)
A contrasting smooth thread, the same weight as the thread of the background fabric, or tapestry wool for Binca.
A tapestry needle.

1. Go over and under 2 threads, working horizontally from right to left. Follow the weave of the fabric.
2. Leave one row free.
3. Come back along the next row, making parallel stitches.
4. Continue for several alternate rows.
5. Go back to the beginning and using vertical stitches, join the stitches to make a line of squares. Work right across each row.
6. Go back to the beginning and decorate the squares, or the spaces between. Work across the **whole** pattern each time, gradually building up the decoration, rather than working on one small area, finishing it and moving on.

    One area of pattern might be built up to create a dark area, with a dense pattern of stitches, one might be lightly patterned and sparse.

    A thick thread gives a darker pattern than a fine thread, so use various weights of thread to give contrast.

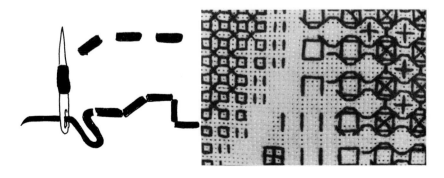

Use graph paper to work out patterns, thinking of the lines as the weave of the fabric, and the spaces as the holes between. Binca canvas is only used in this exercise because it is easy to see and count. When you have mastered the technique, use a finer evenweave, with a variety of smooth yarns.

Traditionally, this technique is known as **blackwork** and it was used in the past to decorate clothes and artefacts with these lovely regular patterns. Today, the technique is often used to create light and dark areas, and is often combined with areas of applied net or spraying.

Stitch patterns, whether on the surface, like couching and straight stitch, or counted like darning and darning patterns can be used as filling stitches (to pattern an area within a shape) or as a background pattern.

All stitch patterns can be regular or irregular, depending upon the effect you wish to create.

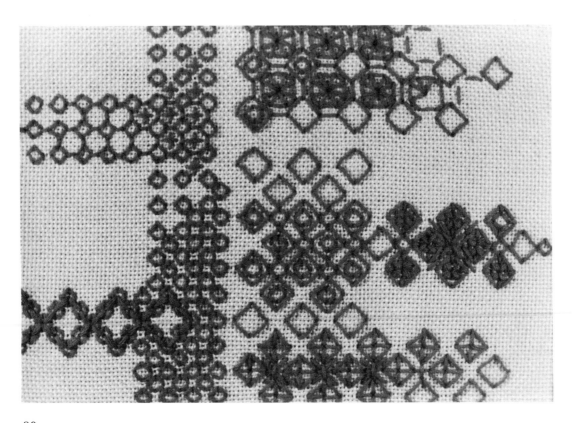

ASSOCIATIONS:

Grids, lines and the man-made environment

Simple design ideas based on using and manipulating straight lines to create patterns can be used successfully in embroidery. How can this method of design be related to looking at the environment as a source of ideas for embroidery?

A great number of things in the man-made environment are almost completely made up of straight lines, simply because people prefer to stand, walk, work and sleep on a flat surface. Lines of windows in a modern office block and scaffolding against a building are almost pure grid patterns, while bricks, pavements, slates on roofs are all arranged in interlocking grids.

It is valuable to start a collection of specific information on straight lines seen in the environment, adding new ideas as they occur over several months.

What to look for:

1. Buildings of all sorts: factory complexes, particularly heavy industry with chimney stacks; rows of houses, as seen from a high point, or houses on a hillside; warehouses by a river; blocks of flats and housing complexes; areas of office blocks; individual houses of all ages.
2. Details of buildings; windows, and the pattern they make on a house, as well as the pattern of the glazing bars; brick and stone patterns, roof tile patterns and patterns round windows and doors; railings and fences; roof ridges, bargeboards and chimney stacks.
3. Scaffolding, large machinery at roadworks, skips of rubbish, cranes.
4. Collections; piles of bricks, lines of deckchairs, books in a bookcase.
5. Vehicles: cars and buses, trains, lorries, boats.
6. Print: letters, graffiti.

Look at these things as if they were a collection of lines and shapes.

Try to forget what they represent, and just look at the pattern they make.

Ideas from man made environment.

How to collect ideas

1. Draw (see p. 57) paint or crayon. Always carry a small sketch book around, and draw fragments as a reminder. Try to make drawn notes on a more ambitious scale, by drawing from a window, or from a parked car. Drawing in public can be embarrassing even to the most experienced because people come and look, so it is often much easier to join a group or take a friend. Hide a small piece of drawing paper in amongst the pages of a novel. Make notes about colour. It is quite difficult to carry colour in your head, so take a magazine, and match the appropriate colours with the coloured pictures and advertisements. It is also important to make a note of the balance of colour, or how much of each colour there is.
2. Take photographs, either in colour or black and white, as a reminder.

How to use the information you have collected.

You might want to use the whole of what you have drawn or photographed as it is, but this is unusual, and a sketch has almost always to be chopped around to make a satisfactory embroidery. With experience, some people do come to be able to note down more or less what they want to embroider, but this takes much time and a lot of practice.

1. Use two card right angles to look at part of the sketch or picture. This might be a large part, or quite a small area or it might be a tiny piece of a pleasing pattern. The important thing is that the chosen part makes an attractive and balanced composition, and that you like it enough to want to embroider it.
2. Small motifs or patterns on buildings can be picked out and repeated side by side to make a border pattern. This can also be very successful, using letters either taken from a book, or copied from some graffiti on a wall. The motif can be used either standing up, upside down or sideways, or a mixture of all three, and with some experimentation, very interesting borders can be built up from very simple shapes.
3. Work some stitch samplers from the sketches or photographs. Do this informally, on a piece of white fabric with a range of grey threads, trying to create the patterns and shapes. Use stitch

textures or blackwork patterns or filling patterns to create areas of light and dark.

See how the colour will look on the fabric by painting over the stitches with watercolour, or drawing a rectangle and blocking in the areas of colour with pieces of fabric.

Try out some areas of the design in different ways, for example by using stitch textures, or by using stitch patterns on evenweave fabric, or by applying areas of net, chiffon or organza and stitching over the top.

It is by looking, collecting and stitching that you get ideas. Embroidery is one of those things you cannot do in your head.

Bottles, blackwork.

"Magic carpet." Machine and hand embroidery on layers of transparent silk chiffon.
MARY YOULES

A larger project: Making a sampler of a house

Making an embroidery or sampler of the place in which you live is appealing and can be very decorative. It is also easy to go out from time to time to look at the source material.

A project like this can be tackled from a number of different angles; for example it might be a straightforward front view of a house or a block of flats, or it might be just one window with a glimpse of an interior, or a balcony with plants and the washing on a clothes dryer. Other occupants of the house might be included or trees or plants from the garden, the family pets, a windowbox, a greenhouse or a piece of furniture. This sort of embroidery is strictly decorative, so everything is arranged in a pleasing pattern, rather than in a natural way, and the proportion of objects is not important.

Many of these types of sampler have a border pattern, and it is a good idea to think of the age of the building and make use of other patterns in the house, on tiles, fireplaces and on plaster and wood. Although modern houses are not always highly ornamented, it is possible to use the triangular shape of a roof elevation, the plan of a house on the ground or a doorway to make a border pattern, and the lines of windows in modern flats are interesting. Ideas can also be taken from wallpaper borders, fabric and tiles.

There is no reason why the whole sampler should be embroidered. The house itself might be a photograph or a drawing mounted within a canvas garden border, or the house might be embroidered in surface stitchery with a paper border. Photographs of the occupants might be included, and so on.

How to begin:

1. Because embroidery is flat, choose an angle straight on to the building, so that perspective does not become a problem. It is helpful to look through a rectangle cut in card for this isolates the particular area to be included. A cardboard slide carrier is ideal for this.
2. Make a rough diagram, getting the angles, the big shapes and areas, and the proportions only. A photograph can be a help, but looking and recording as well gives a much more satisfactory result.
3. Decide which technique you wish to use and choose the background fabrics and coloured yarns, fabric paints etc. The colours chosen depend on what time of day, what time of year you wish to show. The weather conditions are very important, and create a mood.
4. Decide on the size. Some techniques take much longer than others, and a canvas embroidery or areas of very close textured surface stitchery will take much longer than a machine embroidery for instance. A large canvas embroidery can take months or even years to complete.

5. Trace the main areas of the design on tracing paper, then reduce or enlarge the design to fit the chosen background.
6. With the help of photographs, and by going out and looking, decide how each area is to be textured, patterned and coloured, or left empty. Use experiments and stitch technique samplers to help you decide. Work out the border pattern.
7. Transfer the design onto the background, using a suitable technique. (see p 25). If necessary, support the background with a piece of washed calico or sheeting. Stitch the two fabrics together with lines of tacking stitch about 5cm. apart, going both vertically and horizontally. The weave of both fabrics should run the same way.
8. Keep a piece of calico or sheeting to pin over the embroidery when you are not working on it, to keep it clean.
9. Always finish the embroidery. Everyone feels rather let down after the excitement of choosing the threads and solving the problems of the design when they find they still have a lot of empty space to fill. Sometimes the embroidery only starts to work with the last few stitches, or even when it is mounted. It is a good idea to put a finished embroidery in a drawer for a week or two, then bring it out and see it with new eyes.

House sampler: canvas and appliqué.
ANNE WESTCOTT

Left: House sampler. Surface stitches, paint, paper border.

More Surface Stitches

It would seem on first looking at a stitch dictionary that there is a bewildering number of complicated stitches. However, many stitches are so closely related that it is sometimes difficult to see where one ends and another begins. This is clear from the number of variations on straight stitch which have already been shown, and how the direction of the needle and the construction of the background fabric can alter the name of the stitch.

1. **Straight Stitch,** or **Flat Stitch** is also called **Running Stitch,** but a long running stitch becomes **Darning Stitch,** while straight stitches worked in a block of parallel lines is called **Satin Stitch.** When Satin Stitch is worked on canvas in a star pattern, it becomes **Algerian Stitch** and so on. Two straight stitches crossed, become **Cross Stitch,** but if the corners are crossed again, but diagonally, the stitch is called **Rice Stitch. Backstitch, Holbein Stitch,** and **Herringbone Stitch** are all members of the same family.

2. **Looped Stitches:** This is a group of stitches where the yarn is looped round the point of the needle in every stitch.

   One of the most well known is **Blanket Stitch.** This is worked horizontally from left to right, but compare it with **Cretan Stitch** worked first from one side, then from the other, and **Feather Stitch** which appears to be almost exactly the same except that the angle of the stitch is slightly different. Try some of these looped stitches.

3. **Chained Stitches:** These stitches are also looped, but form a closed chain, and include **Chain Stitch** and **Detached Chain Stitch** (Lazy-Daisy) as well as some beautiful but less well known stitches like **Twisted Chain, Rosette Chain** and **Open Chain.**

4. **Couching:** This has already been mentioned as the easiest way of holding down a thick or an uneven thread. There are several variations.

5. **Knotted Stitches:** These are formed when the thread is wound several times round the point of the needle, which is then taken back through the fabric in almost the same place, leaving a knot of thread on the surface. **French Knots** and **Bullion Knots** are well worth trying as they make a lovely raised texture.

6. **Composite Stitches:** or stitches built up from two or more

stitches. Many stitches can be laced with another yarn to make them more attractive, and by working stitches on a foundation of straight stitches, a very raised texture can be produced. Laced Stitches include **Pekinese Stitch, Interlaced Band** and **Maltese Cross. Raised Chain Band** and **Raised Stem Stitch** are both worked on a foundation of straight stitches arranged like a ladder.

All the stitches have evolved over centuries, as people have experimented with stitches on new materials and have tried to vary the way a stitch has been done.

Making use of a Stitch Dictionary

These books are collections of all possible stitches, and some also include canvas work stitches and stitches for the techniques like Drawn and Pulled Thread embroidery.

Each stitch is set out as clearly as possible so that it is easy to see from the diagram how each stitch is done. It is then up to the reader to interpret the stitch, to experiment with it and see what it will do.

Choose one or two stitches from each section mentioned on the previous page and work on each.

1. Start by just getting to know how to work the stitch easily. Get into the rhythm of the stitch.
2. **Lines and Borders:** Many stitches make a definite line, and several

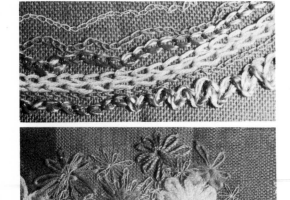

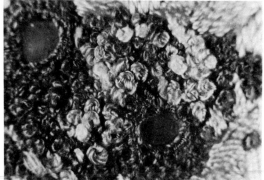

Above: French knots. MARGARET RIVERS

Above left: Chain stitch.
Left: Detached chain stitch.

88

rows of the same stitch can be worked to form curving lines, or intertwining lines. Sometimes one stitch can be worked over another. Two different stitches might be combined or one stitch might be laced or threaded with another yarn. Stitches like Blanket and Chain can be used to couch down a thick yarn or string.

See the contrast of very fine and very thick yarns worked next to each other. Contrast yarns and stitch sizes. Some stitches might be very small, some very big.

3. **Making Patterns:** Make regular patterns by criss-crossing lines of stitches, then decorating the spaces created with other stitches. Some stitches can be worked in circles, some stitches can be worked detached like **Detached Chain Stitch, Fly Stitch** and **Sheaf Stitch,** and arranged in borders and circles.

4. **Making Textures:** Work some stitches in dense blocks or heaped across one another, upside down, going at different angles and in different directions. Make stitches both even and uneven, to create interesting textures. Work small stitches over larger stitches.

Always try stitches in a variety of yarns, even strips of fabric and also try stitches on several backgrounds, like evenweave, transparent, patterned and hand printed, etc.

These experiments might be worked over months or even years as most embroiderers find that they need continually to explore stitches.

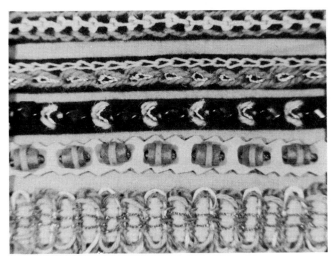

Stitches worked together.

Open chain stitch.

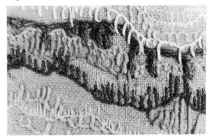

Blanket stitch.

Design with curved line

Everything we see around us seems to be composed of either straight or curved lines, or a mixture of the two. For the purpose of design for embroidery, it is advantageous to separate the two, trying out each in a number of ways so that the different line patterns become familiar.

Some experiments with curved lines

You will need:
Cartridge paper, coloured paper, ruler and scissors.
Pencils and colours.
The exercises can be done within a rectangle, or drawn freely.
1 Draw a curved line, either vertically, horizontally or diagonally. The line might be very curved or only slightly curved.
2. Draw a second line, following the first, but coming close at some points and veering away at others. Continue drawing lines in this way until the area is filled. If the design is within a rectangle, the lines should touch the sides; if not, the area covered should simply look pleasing.

   Try several of these exercises, using colour, crayons, ink etc. to fill in some of the spaces between the lines. Some of the designs will look very much better than others, but do each one as carefully as possible.
3. A variation of this exercise is to take a rectangle of coloured paper and cut a curved line across it. Cut more lines, in the same way as lines were drawn in the first experiments. Arrange the pieces of cut paper on cartridge paper, leaving a space between each. Stick down. More lines might then be added, or the design left as it is.

More experiments with curved lines.

1. Draw a horizontal line about 7–10cm. long. Starting at one end of the line, draw a curved line up, then down to meet the other end of the line, like a cloud pattern.

   Follow this curve with several more lines, some close, some widely spaced, as before.

90

2. Divide a rectangle into two parts with a faint pencil line, vertically. Draw a curved line to the left of the line and another curved line to the right of the line. Each should be different. Draw more lines, filling in the area nearest the side of each rectangle.

3. Divide a rectangle into four or five areas with slightly curved lines from one side of the rectangle to the other on the horizontal. Fill each area with a continuous line following the

shape of the area **OR** leave one or two empty and fill the rest with **vertical** lines, some close, some far apart.

4. Draw a vertical line about 7cm. long. Draw a curved line from top to bottom, sometimes crossing the vertical line, like a snake. Follow the line on the left, side with a parallel line. This will be curved in parts and straight in parts. Follow the line on the right side in the same way.

   These doodling exercises are easy to do and produce some interesting patterns, which might be suitable for embroidery. Use a variety of pens, pencils and crayons to fill in some areas or to pattern some areas.

5. Make similar patterns by cutting into rectangles of tissue paper. Arrange these on a background and stick down.

Design with curved line

Experiments with fabric and thread.

Use these designs to try out new stitches. Some stitches make lines, while others produce lovely textures, and this becomes obvious by using the stitches in different ways. When using a large number of stitches in one sampler, it is a good idea to restrict the colour.

Do several small pieces of work, to try out ideas.

You need:
A variety of background fabrics, including evenweaves and canvas. Threads which match in with the background fabric. Make sure the colours look attractive together.
Embroidery ring, scissors, needle and fabric marker.

Draw out each pattern on the fabric before stitching, using the curved line designs from the previous pages.
Try out some of the following ideas:

1. Embroider along the lines of the design, with suitable surface stitches. Fill in some of the areas completely with lines of stitches. Use a variety of yarns. Leave some areas either empty or sparsely patterned with stitches for contrast.

2. Instead of embroidering lines, fill in some of the spaces with textures or definite patterns, using surface stitches. Use fabric paints and crayons to add colour.

92

3. Try some of the patterns on canvas. Fill in the spaces with canvas stitches. Some of the stitches will be too big to fit in right up to the edge, so fill in the gaps with tent stitch in the same colour.
4. Using evenweave fabric, fill in some of the spaces with either darning or blackwork patterns. Like canvas patterns, some of the blackwork patterns will not fit exactly right up to the edge so allow the pattern to fade out at the line and the pattern in the next area to start taking over.
5. Cover a sheet of paper with transfer fabric paint or crayon. Cut curved line patterns across the paper, arrange and stick down. These patterns can be printed on synthetic fabric, then decorated further with stitches.
6. A cut-out paper pattern can be used as a stencil, for spraying paint onto fabric. Again, the pattern can be decorated with stitches.

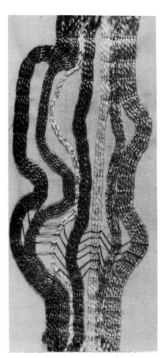
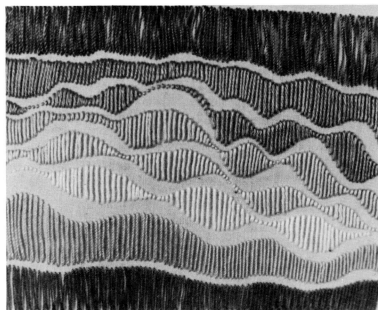

ASSOCIATIONS:

Curved lines and the natural environment.

Landscape.

Many of the patterns formed by curved lines are similar to the pattern of landscape in hilly country.

Holiday photographs, pictures in holiday brochures and geographic magazines are all useful as design sources, but better still is a landscape sketched from life. Although sketching and painting take up quite a considerable time, even a very rough sketch is valuable, with photographs as back-up to reinforce the memory of shapes and patterns. Try at the same time to make a note of the colours and the mood created by the scene. Use the coloured pictures in a magazine to match colours as suggested on page 83. Note the shapes made by the lines of the landscape and the direction of the lines of the texture and pattern in each shape. Think of possible stitches, fabrics which might be applied and stitched over and background fabrics. By making sketches and taking notes, it is possible to collect information for a future embroidery which can then be carried out at a later date:

Embroidering a landscape

1. Decide which part of the picture or sketch you wish to embroider. It might be the whole scene or just a part, or it may be a fragment which happens to have an interesting pattern or texture. Trace this off on tracing paper.
2. Decide on the technique. This might be surface stitchery, canvas work or a mixture of applied fabrics and stitches. It might be a machine embroidery, with parts coloured in paint or crayon, or it might be a technique like blackwork.
3. In view of the technique, decide on the size of the finished work, and enlarge or reduce the design on another sheet of paper. Look at the original sketches, photographs and information on colour and indicate on the design the DIRECTION of the texture or pattern lines in each main area, choosing suitable stitches either from samplers already done, or by trying out small areas of stitches on a piece of spare fabric.

4. Assemble the background fabric, the yarns, pieces of fabric etc. and lay them out on the design, choosing darker tones of colour for the darker areas and lighter tones for the lighter areas. Make sure the balance of colour and tone (light and dark) is going to

"Northumberland" drawing.

look right. It is a good idea to pin the design and colours onto a board and stand away from them to get a better idea of the all over effect.

5. Mark out the design on the background fabric.
6. Sometimes, even at this stage, one or two minor changes have to be made, but with careful preparation, the embroidery should proceed smoothly.

Keep all the sketches and design together in a plastic wallet.

Small gardens

Flower beds are usually planned with small plants in front and taller plants behind forming layers of colour, and a rockery is a landscape in miniature. Areas of pattern are made by the masses of round, conical, starry and spiky flower heads, set off by lines of straight stalks and the darker patterns of the leaves. Many gardens are set out with paving, brick edgings, wooden and plastic lattice, as well as walls and tubs and pots, and these formal grid and linear patterns contrast with the informality of the plants and bushes.

Canvas embroidery is traditionally formal, working stitches over counted threads to create the surface pattern and texture, but some delightful results can be produced by using surface stitches like French knots and bullion knots and detached chain stitch over the canvas stitches to make a more informal decorative effect.

A little garden can be produced by building up gentle curves and filling each with contrasting stitch patterns. Designs can be worked out on paper or directly onto fabric.

You will need:
Coarse evenweave linen, or fine canvas.
Brightly coloured silk and fine cotton yarns. Fabric paints.
Tapestry needle and small tambour ring.
Cartridge paper, pencils and colours.

1. Mark out the design on the fabric. This sort of simple design can be done with lines of tacking stitch **OR** the design can be painted on the fabric and the stitches worked over the paint, leaving some areas painted but not stitched.
2. Work a formal baseline. Refer to the canvas stitches on page 65.
3. Work the flower shapes. These might not fit exactly into the areas marked out, but can be as near as possible. Vary the size of the

stitch pattern shapes. Use some canvas stitches like eyelets, leaf stitch and some surface stitches.

4. Add the leaf areas, then fill in the stalks with straight stitch.

Go on to more complicated arrangements by looking at plantings in parks and gardens, and making sketches and notes, and look at pictures in gardening magazines, books and seed catalogues.

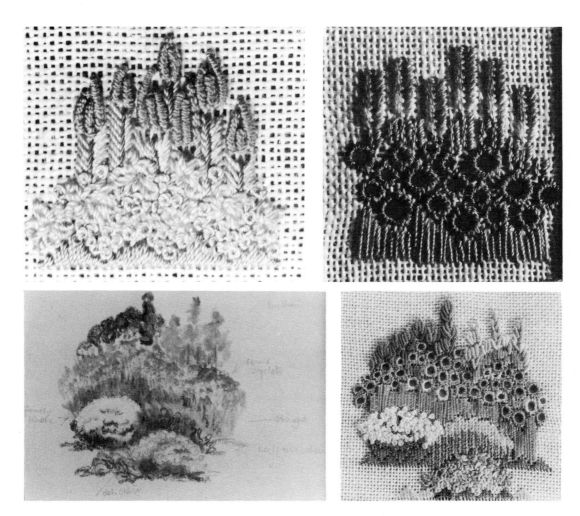

Shape or form

One of the reasons we are able to recognise an object is because of its shape. An embroidery based only on an interesting texture or on a range of beautiful colours must fit into some sort of form or boundary, since everything must begin and end somewhere. For some people, texture and pattern are of paramount importance while for others, shape and form are most significant and they need to represent what they see in a definite form. A balance of form, pattern and texture and colour usually go towards making the most successful embroidery.

Geometric shapes:

Shapes like squares, circles, diamonds, scales and ogees are a useful resource for design, and the innumerable patterns they make, both in informal groups or in grid and border patterns have been used over the centuries and are still being used today. Make a collection of sketches and pictures of geometric shapes in other media: stone, ceramic, ironwork, textiles, print and wood.

Design with geometric shape: Circles

You will need:
Cartridge paper, tissue paper, blotting paper, paints, pencils, ink. Scissors and glue. Tweezers.
1. Drip blobs of ink onto blotting paper. Make splatter and cluster patterns like spilt milk. Add lines by drawing from one edge of the splatter to the other, but avoiding the splatter on the way, as water avoids a stone, or in the form of lines on wood going round a knot. Continue to draw lines, following the first line.
2. Drip a lighted candle onto paper, so that the grease makes similar patterns to the ink. Go on to making trails of candle grease, circles and ovals and spirals of dots of grease. With a paint brush and paint, colour across the grease prints. Not only will the paint run off the wax, but more dots of paint will be created to give texture.
3. Cut numbers of circles (freehand) from tissue paper, in different

sizes. Arrange these in various ways:

a) Overlapping in lines to form a regular pattern.
b) In a splattered pattern with the large circles in the centre and the smaller ones towards the edge.
c) In a spiral, with the larger circles in the middle and the smaller towards the outside.

When you are satisfied with these arrangements, stick them down. **NOTE: On sticking tissue paper.** It is much easier to glue an area of background, and place the tissue paper shapes with the tweezers, rather than spreading glue onto the tissue paper itself.

4. Cut large circles in tissue paper. Divide each in different ways.
   a) Cut into segments.
   b) Divide by cutting horizontal straight or curved lines.
   c) Cut in horizontal and vertical lines.
   d) Cut out the centre of the circle, and the centre of that circle and so on.
5. Cut a large circle and fold into either four or eight. Cut pieces out from the sides and the end, open out and stick down.

There are many variations on these themes. Always think of the space created by the cuts and the spaces between the stuck-on shapes. The space round the stuck-on shapes is as important as the shapes themselves. Add lines to the patterns, following the line of the design, not introducing more pattern otherwise the whole appearance will become too messy.

Exercises 3, 4, 5 can also be carried out with other geometric shapes.

Design with geometric shape. Experiments in embroidery.

Some of the designs will be suitable for embroidery, some not at all. Only experience will tell which designs translate successfully into fabric and thread, so do not feel depressed if some do not work. Before beginning, consider some of the following:

1. Does the technique fit the design? A design which looks beautiful on canvas might look indifferent when worked in surface stitchery. It is valuable to try out one or two small designs in different techniques.
2. Would the stitches look more attractive decorating **only** the shape, or **only** the background? This is called **VOIDING**. Sometimes one looks very much better than the other. If both the background and the shapes are embroidered, be careful not to make the work look too fussy.
3. Have you chosen the most suitable stitch? Some stitches make more satisfactory lines, others better textures. Stitch samplers are very helpful in deciding which to use.
4. Is there a good balance between the design and the background? Although it is important to leave a border round an embroidery for mounting, the design should be well placed, with not too much space round the edge, but not so little that the embroidery looks too big.

Try some small scale experiments, using circles, either following some of your designs from the previous pages or working freely on some of the exercises listed below.

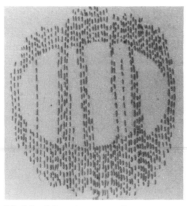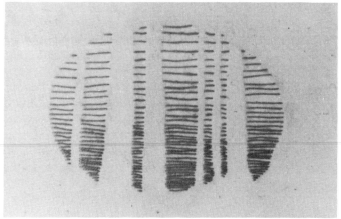

Voided background.

You will need:

A variety of background fabrics and matching yarns.

Embroidery ring, needles, stiletto, fabric marker.

1. a) Make dots and circles in splatters and clusters, spirals and rows. For example, combine French knots beads and small straight stitches in several weights of smooth yarn.

   b) Work surface stitches in circles in sunburst patterns. For example fly stitch, cretan stitch, blanket stitch, chain stitch.

   c) Work stitches in a whirlpool effect, so that the stitches give a feeling of movement.

   d) Working from the centre, build up a large circle with several stitches, or use applied fabrics with stitches.

2. a) Cut out circles in transparent fabrics like net, chiffon, nylon, organza and organdie and arrange on a background, some overlapping. Attach with clusters of stitches rather than rows or stitches round the edge. These fabrics look quite acceptable with a raw edge.

   b) Use very thick fabrics like felt in the same way.

3. Print or paint a pattern of circles, using the same sort of ideas used with cut paper. Decorate some shapes with stitches, or decorate the background with stitches.

At all times, keep the design simple and uncluttered. Ideally there should always be a balance between heavy and sparse stitchery and dark areas of colour and texture, even on a small sampler.

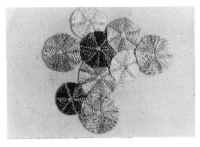

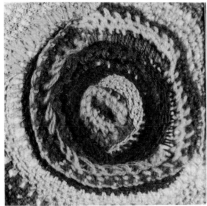

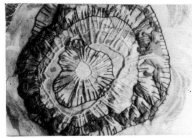

MARGARET RIVERS

ASSOCIATIONS:

Shape and line, colour and pattern, and the natural environment. Natural objects.

Leaves and flowers, shells and stones, bark and feathers can all be seen in terms of shape and pattern, colour and texture. Notice the shape of a feather, the pattern of a leaf, the subtle colours of a shell and the structure and pattern of a cross section of a fruit or vegetable.

1. Look carefully at one of these objects, and notice the shape. As the object is turned, the shape changes so that everything has an infinite number of shapes. It is up to you to choose the angle you prefer. Draw the object from several angles. Notice the shadows on the object and draw these as shapes within the main shape. Arrange several of these shapes, drawn from different angles in a group.

2. Look at some of the objects as they are grouped together naturally. Notice how fruits hang on a tree, how plants grow, the direction of each leaf and twig, the angles of branches, the shapes of each individual flower, and how it grows in a bunch of flowers, the shape of the whole plant. Try to draw or cut out shapes and arrange them in a group. Take into account the angles of growth, and the natural disposition of each.

3. Look then at the pattern of lines within a shape. How do the main lines of the pattern follow the shape of a shell or a feather? Draw main line patterns within shapes.

4. Look at the line patterns in different small areas of the object. Draw what you see and compare these patterns and textures with the exercises with dots and circles and lines. It is surprising how similar they are.

5. Look at the colour of the object and pick out a range of at least twelve colours, using paints and magazine pictures. Natural objects are interesting and decorative subjects for embroidery, either in the mass, or in a group, or individually, or by using just a small area as the basis for a design.

It would be almost impossible to embroider every detail of something as complicated as half a melon, for example, and the looking and recording ensures that you choose what you think are

  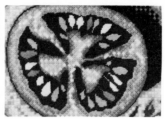

Sketch   *Collage*   *Tomato. Canvas work.*

the most important points to interprete in embroidery. Even the initial drawing has to be simplified into a design suitable for stitches and fabric. You have to capture the shapes and the patterns, but arranged in a pleasing and simple composition. You cannot show every single pip in the melon, or every little line of the membrane, but it is possible to show a melon shape and colour, to show with a few seeds the pattern of all the seeds and the way they grow, to give an impression of the texture without showing every little line.

A design for embroidery can be simplified further by making a cartoon in fabric collage. When making this, refer back to the source of the design, rather than the drawing.

Daisies by PEGGY FIELD.   *Herbacious border at Parham I by VICKY LUGG.*

103

For this you need:

Some natural fabrics like muslin, tarletan, hessian, cotton and threads. These should be in the colours of the object of the collage. Tweezers. Wallpaper paste. Card covered with hessian.

1. Cut out the main shapes in fabric, or dip pieces of fine fabric into the wallpaper paste, and push into shape on the card, while wet. Wallpaper paste is much easier to use than fabric glue, because the fabric is completely soaked, and therefore more pliable.

2. Use the yarns to make the main line patterns and use the tweezers to push the threads in position on the wet fabric. Allow to dry. More colour can be added with fabric paint.

   This cartoon will give a good impression of the general main areas of colour and pattern on the embroidery. Cartoon, drawings and stitch samplers are then used as reference when working the final embroidery.

Embroidery with people.

For the purposes of embroidery, a person is also a shape, textured, coloured and patterned, just like any other natural object. However, it seems difficult to capture a definate shape because people are constantly changing, moving around, bending and turning. It is helpful to take photographs of groups of people, or to look at family photographs where groups of people are arranged formally. Photographs in magazines are also useful, although fashion plates, where models are arranged and pinned into place do not give a true impression of what people really look like. Real people are far more likely to be bundled up in clothes, rather like rectangles with arms and legs.

   Look at yourself in the mirror and notice the proportions of the human body.

1. How many times would the head, measured from chin to the top of the head, fit into the rest of the body? Draw this out on paper as a rough plan, using a rectangle to indicate the head measurement.

2. How long is a hand compared with the foot and the face?

3. Where do the fingers end?

4. Where are the waist, elbows, knees and hips in relation to each other?

   The proportions of the body are important, and knowing them

makes it much easier to depict a person with confidence.

Look at the way each joint bends. The angle of the limbs is also important. Draw diagrams of yourself bending, sitting, balancing in various positions, as if you were a stick man.

Go on to comparing your proportions with those of people in photographs. They will be very similar to other adults. When you are making these sort of notes, try to think of yourself as a collection of shapes, lines and patterns. Cut or tear body shapes in paper, or cut in fabric, very simply.

1. Try to depict a group of people standing in a crowd by cutting ovals of pale coloured fabric and embroidering features, lips, eyes, noses and mouths. Each person seems to come to life as each head takes on its own personality. Find the position of the features by looking at yourself in a mirror. Add hair, moustaches etc. Push the faces close together to give the feeling of a crowd.
2. Try to show a group of people standing talking or dancing or

Machine appliqué

playing a game by cutting out simple shapes like rectangles, ovals and squares. Try to create an overall impression rather than a lot of detail at this stage.

Everything, both natural and man-made can be seen as a collection of lines, shapes, pattern, texture and colour. Some shapes are extremely complicated and change all the time, like running water, waves on the sea, birds in flight and animals and people on the move. Other shapes are simple and static like stones, fungus, fruits and vegetables. Although many objects have fragmented patterns and textures, others have bold, interesting patterns which are easy to see and copy. Colour is everywhere, often so subtle that it is unnoticed unless you really look and analyse, but at other times it is stunning, exciting and vibrant.

From a teeming, complicated environment, embroiderers, like all artists and craftsmen, have to choose and abstract some small part

Appliqué and stitching. ANN FARTHING

which interests them and which can be shown in fabric and thread. Which angle captures just the right interpretation. How can it be shown? Which technique would be best? A shape might be shown alone, as a silhouette, or repeated over and over as a border pattern, while the texture might be taken and used as an abstract decoration. A colour scheme taken from a cabbage, or a bunch of sweet peas might be used for a ribbon weaving, or a stitch sampler and so on.

When you look at anything in the environment ask yourself not only

1. How could a naturalistic embroidery be designed and carried out? but also
2. Could any of the shapes or a group of similar shapes be used? Could a shape be used to form a repeating pattern or an all-over pattern within a grid.
3. How might the whole design be used with different materials, and using different techniques.
4. Could a part of the pattern be used alone? Might it be used to decorate another shape, a square, a circle or a diamond.
5. Could all or some of the colours be used together in a border pattern or on a patterned shape.

The shape, texture and colour of an object can be used together and separately again and again in different ways and combinations and that is why it is so important to continue to collect information in the form of drawings, photographs, colour schemes, stitch samplers and experiments which might be useful later as the basis of a design for embroidery.

Mounting and Presentation

In the past, before the advent of machines and cheap embroidered clothing, embroidery was almost always used in functional way to decorate clothes and artefacts. Today, a piece of embroidery does not have to have any useful function; it might be beautiful, amusing, striking or disturbing like any other work of art and although people still embroider clothes, these are often regarded as wearable works of art and only worn on special occasions. The important point to remember is that suitable materials should be chosen for the function of the embroidery. Cushion covers should be washable; embroidery on clothes should not have long threads which catch on things; canvas seats and mats should not be so three dimensional that they are uncomfortable to use.

A piece of embroidery which might have taken several months to design and hours to work, deserves to be well presented. The way this is done depends on the embroidery. A small fragment might be best displayed in a simple perspex box while a large canvas work might need to be mounted and framed.

Ironing

Never iron onto the front of a piece of embroidery, as this will flatten the stitches. Instead, pin onto a thick piece of blanket face down, cover with another piece of cloth, and press carefully. A damp cloth can be used on fabrics other than silk which might show a watermark.

Stretching

Canvas embroidery and embroidery which is very puckered and creased and cannot be ironed flat might need to be stretched into shape.
1. Use a piece of wooden board slightly bigger than the embroidery. Make a rectangle by drawing lines parallel with the edges of the board. The rectangle should be about the same size as the embroidery.
2. Cover the area within the rectangle with two or three layers of damp blotting paper.

3. With the right side of the embroidery facing **UP**, take the top right hand corner and nail to the top right hand corner of the rectangle with a panel pin.
4. Pull the top left corner or the embroidery to the top left corner of the rectangle and pin down.
5. Nail across every 2cm. pulling the fabric into shape.
6. Continue nailing down the other sides and across the bottom, until the embroidery is pinned out flat.
7. Leave in a warm place, until the blotting paper is completely dry, then remove the pins.

   This method can be used to remove quite stubborn puckers in canvas and linen, hessian and cotton, and a badly distorted fabric can be retrieved.

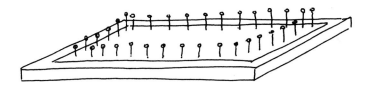

Lacing

An embroidery or a fabric mount to which an embroidery is to be sewn, needs to be laced over cardboard or hardboard to hold it smooth and in position. This technique is also useful when making embroidered boxes. The hardboard or cardboard should be 1cm. larger all round than the embroidery.
1. Prepare the hardboard by sticking one or two layers of terylene wadding on the front. Use a very small amount of glue. Allow to dry.
2. Turn in the embroidery about 1cm. all the way round. Machine .
3. Place the embroidery face down on a piece of clean paper then lay the hardboard wadding side to the back of the embroidery. Pull each corner round over the board, mitre into place and pin securely.
4. Using strong thread or fine string, and starting from the top middle, take a stitch. Take a stitch from the bottom middle and work outward, picking up from the top, then the bottom, so that the thread criss crosses the back. When the thread runs out, knot on another piece. Go back to the middle and work out to the other side. Do not pull tight at this stage.

5. Lace the sides in the same way.
6. Make sure the embroidery is in the right position and carefully pull the lacing tight.
7. Finish off securely, and oversew the mitres.

The fabric should not be pulled out of shape, but fit snugly over the board. The wadding will give a slightly padded effect, which will get rid of any stray wrinkles.

Small embroideries can be laced onto card in the same way.

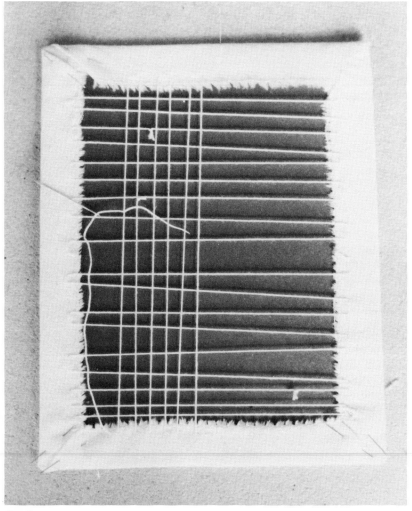

Lacing.

Mounting

The appearance of an embroidery is greatly enhanced by a card or fabric mount. A mount will also hide untidy edges etc. The type used depends on the embroidery.

Card mounts

Card is available from many art shops and comes in a wide range of colours, and it is important to choose a colour which shows the embroidery to best advantage. Grey with a tinge of the dominant colour in the embroidery will look harmonious. Bright and dark colours should be used with caution, although they can occasionally look stunning. Take the embroidery to the shop and try it against the available colours.

The mount should be either the same width all round or slightly wider at the bottom, and can be either narrow or wide. It is a good idea to look in picture galleries, fine art and gift shops and embroidery exhibitions to see the various styles.

1. Cut the mount on a board, or cutting board, using a very sharp craft knife and a ruler. A steel rule is best. It is important that the cutting lines and angles are absolutely accurate, so use a T-square if available, but remember that an ironed newspaper has 90 degree corners, too.
2. Work out the dimension of the hole to be cut on the BACK of the card, then push a sharp point through at each corner and cut on the front. The hole should be about 5mm. less than the work.

Equipment for mounting.

3. Place the embroidery behind the mount and attach with masking tape or brown paper tape.

Fabric mounts

1. A fabric can be laced to a padded board (see Lacing) and a piece of embroidery can then be sewn on it with slip stitch.
2. A small mount can be made entirely in fabric by cutting out a mount in iron-on interfacing, ironing onto the back of the fabric, then cutting and folding over the interfacing. Iron and stick down with double sided iron-on interfacing (Wunderweb).
3. A card or hardboard mount can be covered with fabric by the same method used with the interfacing. First mark out the hole to be cut by machining twice round the shape of the hole. Make sure you are working with the grain of the fabric. When the fabric is cut, the machining will stop any fraying. Fold the fabric to the back of the mount and either stick or lace across. It is a good idea to have a practice run with these methods to iron out any problems before working on a larger scale.

Framing

Embroideries can be glazed and framed in a conventional way, although many people prefer to use more informal methods.
1. Commercial frames: Small, ready made picture and photograph frames, sold at stationers, specialist craft suppliers and department stores are often suitable for embroidery. Individually made frames are very expensive, and it is therefore a good idea to consider the framing when planning an embroidery, and perhaps alter it a few centimetres to fit into a commercial frame.
2. Clips: Embroidery can be effectively mounted on fabric, then sandwiched between glass and hardboard which is then clipped together. Glass and clips are available at glaziers or sometimes from hardware or DIY shops.
3. Box mounts: Acrylic plastic box mounts are ideal for a piece of embroidery, or a group of small pieces.
4. Banners: Embroidery can be presented as a banner or a hanging by adding a fabric border. The borders at the top and bottom should be wide enough to double over to make a tube for a dowel rod.
5. Integral mounts: The mount is embroidered or coloured to

match the embroidery. The frame must be planned at the same time as the embroidery, and it is advisable to put together a trial piece so that any problems are solved at the planning stage.

Plastic acrylic box mount.
DOROTHY WALKER

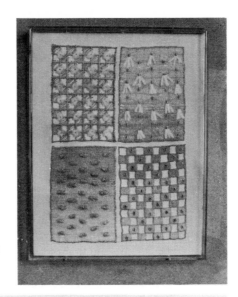

Below: Embroidery between glass and harboard clipped together.

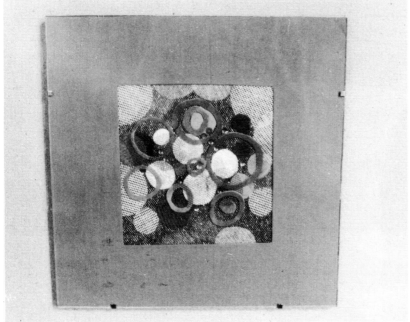

Resources

1. Embroiderers' Guilds: The Embroiderers' Guild welcomes absolute beginners as well as experienced embroiderers. There are branches all over the country. No book can replace a live demonstration, and as well as having the opportunity to learn a variety of techniques and stitches, there is a chance to meet other sympathetic people.
2. Classes: These are set up by local education authorities, who advertise in local papers and libraries. Classes usually begin in the Autumn. Private classes are sometimes held and advertisements can be seen in libraries and specialist shops.
3. Residential Courses: These are advertised in specialist magazines, and in the literature of the college concerned.
4. Books: There are many books on every aspect of embroidery and these can be borrowed from the library initially, and bought if they are particularly useful. Look for books in specialist shops as well as the craft section of book shops.
5. Museums: Embroidery is an old craft, and most museums have a textile department. It is interesting to look at historic embroidery to see how the same stitches are used in a different way and how the function of embroidery has changed. Sections on ethnic and tribal art, which often includes textiles, are full of inspiration and ideas for colours and textures and patterns.

MARGARET RIVERS

Conclusion

I hope that this book has shown that embroidery can be a fascinating medium of self expression for anyone who is willing to try, and not a mystique only open to the chosen few. Embroidery is evolving all the time and there are always new paths to explore both in experimental and creative work, as well as in the more traditional techniques.

A book like this can barely scratch the surface of an interest which captures the imagination of more and more people every year. For many, working with fabric and threads becomes an adventure, an exciting pursuit, even an obsession which can last a lifetime.

Glossary

Motif: an isolated or detached pattern.

Weft and warp: In a woven fabric, the warp threads lie parallel to the edge of the fabric and the weft threads cross at right angles to the warp.

Kapok: A material used for stuffing or padding. A synthetic stuffing could also be used.

Terylene wadding: A thick mat of fibres used as a padding. Stuffings and waddings are available from large haberdashers.

Metallic fabrics and threads: have a proportion of metal lurex or plastic lurex to give a glittery appearance.

Plasticised fabrics: These have a plastic surface bonded to the fabric which gives a wet, shiny look.

Card right angles: similar to the metal right angles used in woodwork. The angle is cut from card. 3– 4cm wide and each arm about 30cm. is a convenient size. Two of these are used together to form a small or large rectangle round part of a drawing or embroidery to isolate it from the rest. This is helpful in choosing a suitable part of the design to embroider.

Surface stitchery: the stitches are worked across the surface of the fabric, rather than as an integral part as in canvas work etc.

Acknowledgements

I would like to thank all the people who have helped me in the preparation of this book, particularly Peter Coleman for taking photographs and giving help and encouragement.

Many thanks are also due to Margaret Rivers for invaluable practical help and advice. Thanks to Anne Westcott, Mary Youles, Ann Farthing, Margaret Rivers, Vicky Lugg, Peggy Field and Dorothy Walker for allowing their work to be photographed and to Ann Farthing for giving permission to use the photograph 'In Chopin's Garden' on page. 106.

The embroidery on p. 106 is reproduced by kind permission of Jan Hassard. The photograph of the sampler on p. 54 is reproduced by kind permission of the Bristol Museum and Art Gallery.

A.C. 1986

Suppliers

Colourist.
Fabric transfer paints.
BA Marketing (Leicester)
8 Latimer Street,
Leicester. LE3 0QE
Tel: 834 202

Details of nearest stockists for Deka
fabric paints
(transfer and direct)

Peggy's Leisure Crafts,
27 Woodland Road,
Tunbridge Wells,
Kent. TW4 9HW
Tel: (0892) 354 72

Details of stockists of Setacolour
fabric paints and pens.

Artemis Products Ltd.
648 Mitchum Road,
Croydon. CR9 3AB

Embroidery yarns of all kinds,
including machine embroidery.

Madiera Threads (UK) Ltd.
15 York Road,
Knaresborough,
North Yorks. HG5 0AF
Tel: (09012) 3555

Machine embroidery threads.

Silken Strands,
33 Linksway,
Gatley, Cheadle,
Cheshire. SK8 4LA

Details of stockists of DMC yarns
for embroidery.

Dunlicraft Ltd.,
Pullman Road,
Wigston,
Leicester. LE8 2DY

Details of all Anchor embroidery yarns
and stockists.

Marketing Services Dept.,
Coats Domestic Marketing Division,
39 Durham Street,
Glasgow G41 1BS

Fabrics paints and crayons,
embroidery frames, fabrics and
threads etc.

Nottingham Handcraft,
17 Ludlow Hill Road,
Melton Road,
West Bridgford, Notts. NG2 6HD

Interesting and exotic fabrics.

Borovick Fabrics Ltd.,
16 Berwick Street,
London W1V 4HP

Lists up-to-date details of suppliers of
requisites for embroidery.

Embroidery Magazine,
P.O. Box 42B, East Molesey,
Surrey. KT8 9BB

Crafts Magazine,
The Crafts Council,
8 Waterloo Place,
London SW1 4AT

PLEASE ENCLOSE A STAMPED
ADDRESSED ENVELOPE TO ALL
SUPPLIERS.

Yellow Pages give details of local
suppliers under 'Art and Craft Suppliers' etc.
These local shops often sell good
ranges of embroidery threads, fabrics,
canvas, paints and crayons etc.
Large department stores carry some
embroidery supplies in the haberdashery department.

Book List

1. Experimenting with stitches:
Stitches: New Approaches by Jan Beaney. (Batsford)
Using Simple Embroidery Stitches by Anne Morrell (Batsford)
Texture in Embroidery by Valerie Campbell-Harding (Batsford)
Constance Howard Book of Stitches (Batsford)

2. Stitch Dictionaries:
Embroidery Stitches by Barbara Snook. (Dryad)
Mary Thomas's Dictionary of Embroidery Stitches
Anchor Book of Embroidery Stitches

3. Colour in embroidery:
Embroidery and Colour by Constance Howard (Batsford)
Embroidery Backgrounds: Painting and Dyeing Techniques by
Pauline Brown (Batsford)
Transfer Printing by Guy Scott (Batsford)
Use of Vegetable Dyes by Thurstan (Dryad)

4. Machine Embroidery:
The Creative Sewing Machine by Anne Coleman (Batsford)
Your Machine for Embroidery by Joy Clucas (Bell and Hyman)
Machine Embroidery: Lace and See-Through Effects by Moyra
McNeill (Batsford)

5. Canvas Work:
Ideas for Canvaswork by Mary Rhodes (Batsford)
Canvaswork by Jennifer Gray (Batsford)

6. Blackwork:
Blackwork by Geddes and McNeill (Dover)
Blackwork by Margaret Pascoe (Batsford)

7. Quilting:
Quilting, Technique, Design and Application by Short (Batsford)
Quilting by Moyra McNeill (Octopus)

8. Ideas for design:
Embroidery and Nature by Jan Messent (Batsford)
Faces and Figures in Embroidery by Valerie Campbell-Harding
(Batsford)

Inspiration for Embroidery by Constance Howard (Batsford)
Landscape in Embroidery by Verina Warren (Batsford)

9. A good comprehensive embroidery book:
Needlework School (Windward)

10.Search Press have published a range of small books in the Needlecraft Series and the following are relevant:
Applique, Canvas Work, Quilting, Stitchery, Blackwork, Machine Embroidery, Embroidery Design.

11.Embroidery Magazine:
This is a quarterly magazine published by the Embroiderers Guild which includes articles on embroidery, details of courses and exhibitions and details of firms which deal in embroidery equipment. For details write to The Embroiderers' Guild, Apartment 41, Hampton Court Palace, East Molesey, Surrey, enclosing a Stamped addressed envelope.